I0186890

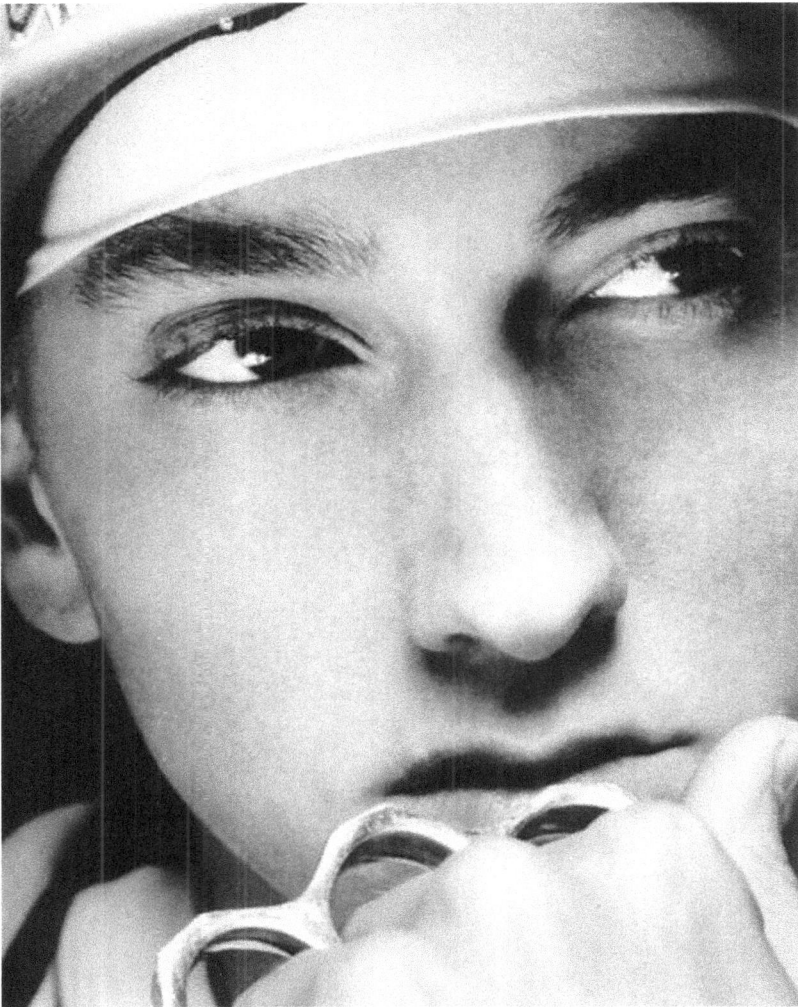

Eminem
and
The Detroit Rap Scene

White Kid In A
Black Music World

Eminem
and
The Detroit Rap Scene

White Kid In A
Black Music World

ISABELLE ESLING

Colossus Books
An Imprint of Amber Communications Group Inc
Phoenix
New York   Los Angeles

Eminem and the Detroit Rap Scene
White Kid in a Black Music World
By Isabelle Esling

Published by:
Colossus Books
An Imprint of Amber Communications Group, Inc.
1334 East Chandler Boulevard, Suite 5-D67
Phoenix, AZ 85048
Amberbk@aol.com
WWW.AMBERBOOKS.COM

Tony Rose, Publisher/Editorial Director
Yvonne Rose, Associate Publisher
Deborah Jackson, Editor
The Printed Page, Interior Design / Cover Layout

ALL RIGHTS RESERVED

No part of this book may be used, reproduced or transmitted in any form or by any means—electronic or mechanical, including photocopying, recording or by any information storage and retrieval system without written permission from the author, except for the inclusion of brief quotations in a review or critical article.

COLOSSUS BOOKS are available at special discounts for bulk purchases, sales promotions, fundraising or educational purposes.

Copyright © 2012 by Isabelle Esling and
Amber Communications Group, Inc.

ISBN#: 978-1-937269-26-5

Dedication

To my sons Marcus and Simon

To Martin Harrell, thanks for your friendship,
support and constructive criticism

DEDICATED TO THE MEMORY OF
BIG PROOF

Acknowledgements

First and foremost, I would like to thank my publisher Mr. Tony Rose, for assisting me and advising me during the whole publishing process. Thanks for helping me perfect this book to the best standards.

I'd also like to thank the whole editorial team at Colossus Books for their help in editing my manuscript.

Many thanks to the Detroit artists I have been in touch with for years. Thanks in particular to all of you who accepted my interview and who gave me more insight about the Detroit scene, sharing your experiences and music with me.

Many thanks to Kevin Bailey aka Dogmatic and to RIP Big Proof in particular, whose knowledge and passion of hip hop has been a big motivator in my life. Many thanks to the whole Iron Fist crew I have worked with for years on the Skrilla Gorillas website. Thanks to Jermaine Harbin aka Uncle ILL for all the knowledge he shared with me and for letting me use his pictures. Thanks to rapper Mu for all the support, thanks to Barry Yett aka DJ Butter for sharing his knowledge and for the use of his pics. Thanks to Omar de Fati for sharing his knowledge of the Detroit scene with me. Thanks to the few insiders who shared with me a lot of very important information.

If I omitted any of you, it wasn't intentional, I am grateful for all the help and support I received from the Detroit scene globally.

Thanks to Eminem aka Marshall Mathers III who has inspired me all these years through his music.

Thanks to the D12 crew for their music; it is also a huge source of inspiration for me.

Big thanks to Gavin Sheridan who got me started as a contributor for Gavin's blog and a blogger at The Eminem Blog.

Thanks to all the readers of The Eminem Blog for your fidelity and contribution. Thanks to Jason Matthews for publishing my interviews in *ILL Mag*. Thanks to the Le Parc Delicatessen team in Stoke Newington. Thanks for your kindness, help and encouragement.

Thanks to all my friends in France and all over the world. A special thanks to Marie Barailler Apisi. Thanks for reading and commenting on my manuscript. Without you, this book wouldn't have been published.

Contents

Introduction

"Life Is a Bitch"

Eminem is probably one of the most talked-about superstars, and, of course, one of the most controversial ones. Whether people like him or not, it is quite impossible to ignore the rapper. A lot of people criticize the talented MC, but wouldn't it be wiser to just listen to his music and take a look at his lyrics?

People should not judge the artist so fast before knowing him better. Coming from a poor background, he's struggled hard while being underground and made his way to become a superstar. His life story is far from being a fairy tale. Bullied at school, experiencing racism on a daily basis, coming from a dysfunctional family with a drug dependant history; Marshall Mathers carried the dream to become a rapper: a dream that was so huge and seemed so foolish to follow that neither his teachers, nor his family took him seriously.

But, as his music teaches us, *"one can do anything he sets his mind to."* His will to succeed would eventually lead him to major success and acclaim.

Marshall Mathers is definitely a white kid lost in a black music world. Eminem used to live in the white hood and in the black hood of Detroit. Most of his friends and collaborators are black.

Growing up on the black side of 8 Mile, because his mom was unable to afford the rent on the white side; the young boy was friends mostly with black folks and focused on the same musical interest as his buddies. Some people might not know that Eminem also lived in Warren, Detroit where he had a bunch of white friends as well. Experiencing both sides of the ghetto provided Eminem with treasured bridges to both cultures.

Eminem's preference goes to black music; a genre in which his immense talent allowed him to become an unusual authority.

During the time Marshall Mathers settled in Detroit; racial tensions divided both black and white communities. A white kid wanting to rap faced a real challenge. Eminem's road to success was far from easy. It required a lot of determination and drive.

You cannot separate Eminem from the over the edge, always in effervescence, Detroit hip-hop scene that is still pretty much unknown to the world. Through his amazing work, Eminem put his hometown on the map and made people realize that hip-hop was very alive in the D town.

Eminem's skin color was a major obstacle that overshadowed his lyrical talent. Eminem had to impose his presence as a white emcee in a black music world and gain acceptance in the Detroit scene.

Despite opinions about the talented rapper, Eminem can indeed be considered a role model for young people, because he proved to the world that if you believe in your dreams strongly enough; you can make them happen.

The goal of this book is to do away with many stereotypes regarding the artist, who is probably one of the most misinterpreted and misquoted emcees in the world, but also to enlighten the reader about an emcee who impacted the world of hip hop like no other.

Think you know all about Marshall Mathers? Eminem is and will remain an enigma to most of us. Unless you know the real Marshall Mathers personally; he remains veiled.

The brilliant artist who proved to the world that skin color doesn't matter in terms of mastering his art; sometimes seems to reveal a lot about himself in his music. However, while composing his astute compound rhymes, the listener will never really know when

Eminem is messing with their head. His subtle uses of syllables in his rhymes transform his music to the highest levels of poetry. Never mind the cusswords: this is street poetry that represents life in the ghetto. In some of his songs, Marshall Mathers reaches the depth of Baudelaire's Flowers of Evil through the intensity and colorful descriptions he combines with a tornado of well chosen words matched with good instrumentals and beats.

You will follow him from his modest beginnings within a dysfunctional family to the successful entrepreneur and world acclaimed talent that he is now.

Chapter 1

The Detroit Hip Hop Scene

I loved Kaos and Mystro, Awesome Dre, Smiley, Prince Vince, Jo to the D, Detroit Box, AWOL, DmW, a lot of local stuff. Awesome Dre's 'Master Of Philology', Merciless Amir's 'A Day Without A Rhyme' and Prince Vince's 'Changes' were some of my favorites. It made me feel proud to be from the D and made the possibilities of making some noise out of the city seem more realistic. I think I owe something to the foundation they all laid, for sure.

—Eminem, *The Hip Hop Connection,* December 2008

If you want to understand Eminem, you have to understand where he comes from. As a matter of fact, he is deeply hip-hop rooted. Most of Eminem's negative critics show their complete ignorance of hip-hop culture. That's also the main reason why they often feel so shocked about his use of a strong language. Some other people think Eminem is just some white artist who tries to imitate black people and who have no idea about life in the hood.

The best way to do away with the many misconceptions regarding Eminem is to follow him into his original place of being: **Detroit City**. Eminem is a white man who totally integrated black culture; he is part of it. He used to live among black folks, was beaten by some of them, made friends with some, and finally grew roots into the culture.

You can't talk about Eminem without mentioning Detroit City, the place that inspired him and made him become the person he is now.

Please note that the artists mentioned in this chapter are a NON EXHAUSTIVE list of artists. It was quite impossible to mention everybody, as the Detroit scene is diverse and huge.

With its racial riots past, its dark reputation of Murder Capital and Cutthroat City, Detroit; a city of cement and the heart of the motor industry is nevertheless, the place of birth for the greatest musicians.

Why this arid place generated so much musical creativity is a mystery.

Famous for its Motown Records artists and techno music; Detroit is also rich in its wide range of hip-hop artists.

Detroit might be a big American city, but the paradox is that its hip-hop scene is quite a microcosm and a macrocosm at the same time. Many emcees know each other, but the numerous artists that compose the scene are quite difficult to figure out individually.

The Detroit hip-hop scene is characterized by its raw sounds and a lot of artistic lyrical creativity. Still underrated and unknown by the mainstream public, Detroit hip-hop is starting to slowly emerge and to show its skills to the world. Before Eminem, very few people were talking about its artists, but the Detroit talent managed to put his hometown on the map. Besides D12, Eminem has truly tried to feature local artists, such as Trick Trick and MC Hush.

Detroit hip-hop is composed of numerous and various talents of all kind. From old school to new school, horror core, acid rap to softer tones, Detroit rap has something for everybody.

While creativity and talents in the D town are undeniable, one of its big weaknesses is its lack of unity. Along with its lack of unity, the lack of local promotion also causes difficulties for underground artists to emerge.

Detroit hip hop scene pioneers

Detroit old school rappers are usually less well known than the other ones. You are entitled to ask why. It is simply because at the time they started making their music; modern technology like the Internet didn't exist. Promoting their music was much more of a challenge than it is now. In addition local radio stations like WJLB weren't really keen on promoting local artists, and they usually gave the preference to mainstream artists from New York.

In the 80's, the Detroit scene was composed of B-Boys and numerous freestylers and battle rappers. Awesome Dre and Big Herc are among Detroit's most valuable old school emcees. Awesome Dre's dark vocals totally fit with his rhythmic instrumental background. His Ice T like voice is mixed with original soundtracks and his flow is unbeatable. Awesome Dre is appreciated among hip-hop connoisseurs. He belongs to the generation of legendary emcees who pioneered the Detroit scene. This man is truly a must hear for any hip-hop lover. Anybody who listens to the talented emcee will certainly enjoy Awesome's Dre's Top Choice track taken out of his very first album (1989) entitled *You Can't Hold Me Back* in which he excels at playing with syllables.

Big Herc was featured on Eminem's "There They Go" song as well as Obie Trice.

Esham, the father of acid rap, who was born in New York and grew up in Detroit represents a rather morbid and scary style in rap music. Whether you like him or not, he influenced Detroit hip-hop to a great extent.

Eminem's mention of acid rap in the Marshall Mathers LP ignited a beef for several years with Esham who took offence because of the following rhyme:

"I ain't "acid rap", but I rap on acid"

Like Esham, Detroit local rappers ICP (Insane Clown Posse);who were actually a great source of inspiration to young Marshall

Mathers, also carried that dark, horror core dimension in their music. Wearing clown masks and using chainsaws in their shows, the group was formed in 1989. Like Cypress Hill, it can be qualified as metal-rap.

There are loads of other names that got the Detroit scene started, like AWOL and Merciless Amir, a Detroit rapper of Lebanese origins, whose music astutely combines Detroit sounds with an oriental flavor.

I had the chance to talk to a true witness of the Detroit hip-hop scene's beginnings. This man's name is Omar de Fati who has a huge passion for hip-hop:

> *I grew up in Detroit, essentially all my life. I moved from Adrian, Michigan, where I was adopted, to Detroit in 1970 at 11 months old. We moved to Fenkell Avenue and Ilene then. After two years living off Fenkell Avenue my family moved to 12th Street and Davidson Avenue I attended Glazer Elementary, Longfellow Middle, and Central High, schools. I was never a music lover before I heard rap music. I didn't like funk, Motown, or the precursors to house and techno (Kraftwerk, etc.) or anything (despite this, I played a relatively great sax). In or around 1983 I was introduced to rap music, but I had already been breakdancing for a year or longer. Although I've grown to love other types of music, including my second musical love—Heavy Metal, rap has consistently been my favorite.*

In an interview, the Detroit homie revealed how the golden age of hip hop started in the 80s and 90s. The artist named K-Stone is in fact better known as Dogmatic, one of Big Proof's closest collaborators. It is quite clear that, in its earliest beginnings, Detroit hip-hop was still in search of its identity.

> *Most well-known local acts seemed more like knock-offs of more popular acts. I remember Kaos and Maestro reminded me of a Public Enemy Clone, Awesome Dre reminded me of a solo N.W.A clone with a little L.L. Cool J flavor, and I thought*

K-Stone was doing the same thing as EPMD and the other early New York 'grimey' acts. Don't take this in a negative way. I mentioned three acts, however, I liked (and still do) all of them. I'm sure Detroit wasn't much unlike other cities outside of New York, with the exception of Florida cities and the West Coast who had their trendsetters in Two Live Crew & Ice T/N.W.A. Some other better known acts from that early era were Detroit's Most Wanted, AWOL, Smiley (aka MC Lyte), Ameer the Merciless (aka Special Ed/Rakim; Ameer was in my opinion; the best of all the Detroit locals during that time.

I believe to this day his song, "A Day Without A Rhyme," is a Hip Hop classic, overall. I still listen to it several times a week. Unfortunately, I wasn't able to follow his career, or even to find out how or if it ended. Oh, I remember Prince Vince and the Hip Hop Force too. These are all late 80s to early 90s era groups. In the mid-90s, so many different experimental styles began to develop in Detroit, it's difficult to discuss in a written format. So I'm basically talking mid to late 80s here. In two main ways Detroit's Hip Hop 'scene' struggled for an identity in two ways:

1. What type of music represents Detroit; and,

2. How to get the music to listeners. Detroit was being influenced by every single style of rap between the late 80s and early 90s. During 1987, while in a juvenile camp I housed this guy's 'Criminal Minded' cassette.

Later, during the 90s, this same guy argues with me that Treach from Naughty by Nature is a better rapper than KRS—while wearing a Heavy D T-Shirt. This is of course anecdotal. The point is; Detroiters had no collective identity as a Hip Hop scene. Detroit's Hip Hop scene also had no infrastructure. The one media that could have (and in my opinion tried) made the biggest difference was the dance show called 'The Scene'. Then later, the spin-off dance show, appropriately named, 'The New Dance Show' often granted access to their audience to local artists. Unfortunately, 'The New Dance Show' primarily played dance mixes and national R&B. So to make this long story end shortly, I'd define Detroit's scene during those years as a 'perpetual infancy'. In the greater scheme of Hip Hop, Detroit is no longer an infant. I'd say it's finally...a rowdy-ass young adult. The problem is, how do you define local?

I remember thinking how cool it must be to be an underground artist in New York and get mad love in New York, but not necessarily anywhere else. I think most artists would be happy with it, and so would I. Well, now there are artists like that from Detroit. There were also nationally known artists from Detroit (setting aside the obvious Em reference since he was an aberration by both race and pure talent) who are essentially better known in other states than here.

*An interview with Omar de Fati, by Isabelle Esling.

Members of Big Proof's first group, 5 ELA, Thyme and Mudd, represent raw rap in its original package. Both emcees are exceptional rhymers who should not be ignored because they are the artisans who made Detroit rap what it is today.

Contemporary Detroit hip hop-rapid over flight of the Detroit hip hop scene

In the 90's, things would change in a positive way. With places like Maurice Malone's notorious Hip Hop Shop, Saint Andrews and The Shelter, Detroit emcees would eventually gather in order to freestyle and to cast their stormy show. It truly introduced a new dynamism into the local scene that became more prolific.

The Hip Hop Shop helped push good hip hop acts who would gain recognition and respect in their free styling sessions, as shown in the 8 Mile movie. Big Proof, who can be considered as the pillar of Detroit's hip hop scene, gave Maurice Malone the concept of the Hip Hop Shop. At first, Maurice Malone wanted to sell clothes, but Deshaun Holton was thinking about open mic sessions, so

why not combine the advantage of both ideas? Denaun Porter*
recalls these times very well:

> *Proof started that. I don't know if a lot of people know the
> history behind that, but Proof gave Maurice Malone the idea.
> Maurice wanted to put a store up. He didn't have a complete
> clothing line, just shirts. Proof was like 'I can sell your clothes'.
> He took the clothes and started selling them; then it turned
> into The Hip Hop Shop.*
>
> *He was like 'I can have open mics'. You'll still have every rapper
> coming in here and on Saturday, they'll be buying clothes.*
>
> *To give you an idea about what it was like, it was maybe a
> 1,200 square-foot room. It had a back room and there was a
> deejay booth way up high where DJ Head was spinning. For
> anybody who rapped in the city, that was the place he had
> to go. It was like the Apollo, the hip hop Apollo of Detroit."*
>
> —*The Hip Hop Connection*, December 2008

At this time people gathered for the fun of making music and
fortunately, the only conflicts between emcees that actually existed
were lyrical.

Because he played a major role in connecting people together, Big
Proof, formerly known by his stage name Maximum, was nicknamed the "Mayor of Detroit". Deshaun Holton was very much
loved in his hometown and appreciated for his excellent free styling
qualities, but the prerogatives attached to his "Mayor of Detroit"
title would also cause a lot of envy and jealousy. The horrible argument that happened on April 11th at the CCC club tragically ended
the talented emcee's life; had to do with his privileged position in
Detroit hip hop.

While the Detroit scene had always been quite eclectic, reuniting
diverse talents such as Raw Collection, Da Ruckus, D12, Royce
da 5.9; it shared the rough Detroit spirit that makes the D town

so different from many other American towns. That coldness is described with lots of Realism in Phat Kat aka Ronnie Cash's *Cold Steel* song.

Detroit doesn't carry the seductive side of sunny LA. Detroit is a cold city of cement where crime rates are high. The place is very industrial; seems dark in its essence. It is nevertheless the largest source of inspiration to Detroit artists. To an external investigative outsider like me; Detroit is a mystery because of the creativity in raises in so many artists who manage to recreate its atmosphere in their lyrics and instrumentals.

When you look at artists like Trick Trick who dip all their inspiration in real facts from the hood, you know there is probably some kind of magic in Detroit City. Detroit might look scary, but it allows gangster rappers to make the best out of their art—which is wonderful.

Presentation of some former Eminem and D12 collaborators

A lot of Detroit rappers became known to the public because of their collaborations with Eminem and D12. However, Eminem and his D12 fellows are like the visible part of the immense iceberg the Detroit scene actually is. Each time music journalists describe it; they fail to mention some artists. It is indeed hard to name everyone or to pay attention to everyone, because you have a macrocosm of single artists contained in Detroit's microcosm.

King Gordy

Eminem fans became familiar with King Gordy thanks to the "8 Mile" movie, in which he incarnates *Big O*. He appears in a quite embarrassing scene, talking to DJ Bushman at the very moment Jimmy discovers Alex cheating on him with Wink.

King Gordy's style is very dark, wicked, and devilish. The gothic rapper, who enjoys calling himself *The Entity*, released an album with the same name in 2003. The talented emcee is truly the Edgar Allan Poe of rap music.

Shady Records artists such as Eminem, Bizarre and Obie Trice have collaborated with King Gordy. The songs "Situations" (featuring Obie Trice), "Time To Die" (featuring Bizarre of D12) and "The Mask" are good examples of their artistic collaboration.

Another key Eminem collaborator is Royce da 5.9. Royce became known to the world thanks to the Bad Meets Evil song on Eminem's Slim Shady LP.

Ryan Montgomery aka Royce da 5.9 is very underrated on a national and international scale. Royce is truly to Detroit what Nasir Jones is to New York. All through the years, this amazing artist has developed a high level of inventive lyrical skills.

On April 12, 2011, after years of estrangement, Eminem signed Royce da 5.9 and his group, Slaughterhouse (Royce da 5.9, Joell Ortiz, Crooked I and Joe Budden), to Shady Records. Eminem also released a song with Royce da 5.9 entitled "Living Proof", in memory of Deshaun Holton in 2011. The song is very rhythmic and it enlightens both rappers' lyrical dexterity.

Bareda aka Mr. Wrong

Bareda aka Mr. Wrong is a Detroit native who started his career with Swifty Mc Vay's first group *Da Rabeez*. Bareda also formed the outstanding *Raw Collection* group along with Swifty. It is also interesting to note that the skilled female emcee, Reddbone (who happens to be Swifty's sister) also belongs to Raw Collection.

Besides his collaborations with D12's Swifty, Bareda released the single "Beat Don't Stop".

Bareda has collaborated with numerous artists, such as: Cee-Lo of the Goodie Mob, Twista, Ja Rule and Memphis Bleek. He also went on tour with Outkast.

In 1999, Bareda joined the Lyricist Lounge Show as a writer and also as an actor. He used to live in LA, but since his return to Detroit City, he took the nickname "Mr. Wrong".

Miz Korona

Miz Korona endorsed the *Vanessa* character in the "8 Mile" movie. The talented rapper who used to go by the name *Pimpette*, now goes by the nickname *"The Laila Ali of Rap"* which is a quite colorful description of what her art represents in the public's eye.

Uncle ILL

Uncle ILL aka Jermaine Harbin was one of Eminem's earliest collaborators. He recalls a very different Eminem from the artist we know now when he first met Marshall Mathers, but who already showed some true motivation for rapping and some excellent verbal skills:

> *When I first met Em he had two dancers, Bill and Fred. I was introduced to him through Fred. I was on some DJ Magic Mike shit. You know; booty bass, techno, house, etc. Em was actually emceeing. He mastered all styles of rhyming. Em knew every single rap album word for word, no lie. Em always wanted to be the best and he did that. He never settled for anything less. Em does what works for him. He may not be the hood rapper or ever spit anything much about the hood other than how he grew up, but he is fire. He came in funny until it was cool to walk with that swagger. Today he's an icon and he deserves every meaning of the word.*

Uncle ILL began rapping at the age of 12. As well as Eminem, Uncle ILL has been influenced a lot by Ice T. He has worked with well-known Detroit artists such as Kid Rock and Eminem. Uncle ILL has collaborated with Detroit rapper MC Hush to create the Da Ruckus group. Uncle ILL has released "If The Beef", "We Shine" with Eminem and "Paperchase2 with D12's Swifty. Uncle ILL has collaborated with producer Mad Chemist and has recorded an album at Silent Records, a company that is directed by Marc Kempf (Eminem's former manager). Uncle ILL has some energetic beats and a strong and entertaining voice.

When I heard the strength of Uncle Ill's song writing and production and his voice is better than ever, I knew this would be a hit.

Marc Kempf * Uncle Ill Interview by Isabelle Esling, featured in *Detroit ILL Magazine*, 2006

DJ Butter aka Barry Yett

DJ Butter, born Barry Yett is a Detroit producer, CEO and a DJ at the same time. His first album was called *"Kill The DJ"* and it featured numerous artists such Eminem, Paradime, Almighty Dreadnaughtz and Royce Da 5'9".

DJ Butter started Deejaying when he was 12. He used to be D12's first DJ in 1999. He has produced more than 200 Detroit artists including MC Korona (the female MC who plays in 8 Mile), King Gordy and Obie Trice.

DJ Butter has released a hip-hop documentary: a DVD that contains interviews of Eminem, Obie Trice and Slum Village. It is entitled the "7 Mile Movie".

"The documentary is about unity before money and after money. I just rap about my pain. I rap about bringing Detroit together. There's a lot of chaos in Detroit." (DJ Butter)

This is how DJ Butter met Eminem:

I used to see him at the Hip-Hop shop in the early 90s all the time. We got to know each other closely by going to the "How Can I Be Down?" music summit in the late 90s. It was me, Proof, Mark Hicks, Bizarre, Eminem and Paul Rosenberg all together trying to get seen and heard out in Miami. I used to see Eminem all the time, in the streets selling his CDs, while I sold my mix tapes. I was one of the first dudes to put him on mix tapes and featured him in my magazine, FUNKFRESHINTHAFLESH

Exclusive DJ Butter interview, Isabelle Esling, 2009

DJ PDog

DJ PDog aka Odell Perry is certainly one of Detroit's hottest DJ's. Odell Perry is known for his astute scratching techniques. He is a close collaborator to Rufus Johnson aka Bizarre.

MC Hush

You can hardly talk about the Detroit underground scene without mentioning Detroit rapper MC Hush.

Mc Hush is one of Eminem's former friends who has witnessed Marshall's pre-rapping time. He has also collaborated with many talented Detroit artists such as Uncle ILL, Shane Capone, Royce Da 5.9, and many more, including Marshall Mathers.

Mc Hush is not just another white emcee trying to make it. In fact, he is an essential component to the Detroit hip hop scene. Mc Hush aka Dan Carlisle is an important witness to Eminem's debut. He also recalls some former beef involving himself, rapper Champtown and Eminem. This is how he got his nose broken by accident:

> *That is a culmination of me and this rapper Champtown's beef with Em back in the day. Em was beefing with Champ because his girl [Kim] was trying to get with him, and I was boys with Champ, so that meant I had a beef with Em. The thing was, yeah, we got into it and, yeah, my nose got broken, but it wasn't because Em punched me or anything. It was because we were fighting and he stood up real quickly and my nose hit his collarbone. It was a total accident. (Mc Hush)*

Mc Hush has recorded "We Shine" with his previous group, Da Ruckus, in 1997. Most of the Eminem lovers enjoy the well-made Eminem/Uncle ILL collaboration. Mc Hush has also recorded with local talents like Royce Da 5.9 and Slum Village. Mc Hush has even collaborated with D12's deceased member Bugz.

Working on various projects, Dan Carlisle signed with Rock City Records, Detroit veteran Shane Capone's label.

"If you want to know what it's really like to be a rapper in Detroit, buy my CD", states Mc Hush.

Mc Hush's discography is quite impressive and includes many talented rappers from Detroit.

Dan Carlisle's previous CD is entitled *Roses And Razorblades*. *Bulletproof* was MC Hush's first Geffen release.

How can we define Mc Hush's style in a few words?

I'd say that it has the raw and typical Detroit sound, a sound that I am used to and that I happen to enjoy very much. It is offensive and dynamic at the same time.

Among the early collaborators who had an impact on Eminem, you could count Detroit emcee Champtown who first gave Marshall Mathers his chance to get featured in the Do Da Dipity video in 1992. Due to a personal dispute regarding Kim, Champtown then turned against Eminem and Proof. His former records contain several Proof disses. The local emcee reconciled with Deshaun Holton before he tragically died in 2006.

A few other Detroit soldiers

Among the Detroit emcees, several groups or artists represent a gloomy and grimy tendency in rap music.

King Gordy and his Fat Killaz group fellow (Marvwon, Fatt Father and Shim E Bango), are all four very proud of their weight, so that they consider *a symbol of sexiness* be classified into Gothic rap. Their scary tales telling, their dark visions of a D town that will soon turn into a horrific nightmare are typical of their music.

Other horrorcore representatives are ICP and Mr. Morbid.

Esham, the father of acid rap's influence is, of course, predominant in Detroit too.

Another genre that is praised in Detroit is *gangsta rap*. Most of those rappers bring hip-hop to its original roots, serving their lyrical dishes very raw and spicy.

Trick Trick

The uncontested talents in Detroit gangsta rap are Trick Trick aka Christian Mathis and his *Goon Sqwad group*. Through years of hard work, since the 90s (some of them are also Big Proof collaborations, like in the *From Death* CD), and his recent collaboration with Eminem, Trick Trick made a name for himself. His amazing piece of work, *The People Vs,* released in 2005, was followed by his excellent The "Villain" album (2008) in which instrumentals, lyrics and flow are well mastered. Trick Trick's raspy voice; the darkness of his themes; his honesty in expression; make him an outstanding artist.

Mu

Mu is also a former Proof collaborator who was befriended with the deceased Mc. Mu tells life in Detroit according to his experience in the Detroit hood. His great sense of reality, his uses of different instrumental composition, his interesting collaborations with local artists such as Journalist 103 (quite unknown from the public, but so much talented), J-Hill and Dina Rae make him stand out of the crowd too.

Mu is Detroit rap brought to its rawest and realest dimensions. His "The Flood" mixtape is definitely worth a look.

It's important to note that Mu was featured in Eminem's Like *Toy Soldiers* video in which he raps against label opponents.

The Detroit rapper is respected on the local scene and is quite an authority there.

To give you a more precise idea of what Mu is about, here is an exclusive interview I did with this excellent Detroit artist in March 2009. In this interview, Mu speaks about his music, his artistic collaborations and the death of Proof.

1. What motivated you to become a rapper?

"I was always pretty good with words and I love challenges, so it just kinda found me when I was about 8 years old."

2. Define your style within a few words.

"Oh my God!! Did you hear what he just said!!!"

3. Your mix tape, "The Flood", is full of roughness, dark elements combined with humor and instrumental creativity. It surely reflects the realness of the Detroit hood. Can you enlighten the readers a little bit about the artistic collaborations you did in your mixtape?

"Well, on "The Flood" I had a lot of very talented friends in the studio at the same time, such as: PROOF, Marvwon, Kuniva, Young Zee, Dina Rae, Ek, Slum Village, D12, etc... So it was pretty easy to find dope mc's to collab' with!!"

4. You did a lot of collaborations with Detroit heavyweight RIP Proof. A few words about them?

"Yeah, we did a lot of songs that weren't released yet but we also won a few awards. Song of The Year for a song titled "BROKEN" featuring Journalist 103. There is a second part to BROKEN called Broken & Fixed That was supposed to go on the Jerry Garcia album (Proof's Album), but we didn't get the paper work finished in time. And a number of other tracks like: That's What's Up (I Miss the Hip Hop Shop Album) "Trife Niggas", "God Made Soldiers" (Unreleased), an Exclusive Track With Proof & Dj Muggs (of Cypress Hill), another Exclusive With Proof & RAS Kass (unreleased) etc...I could go on & on!!!"

5. Proof's death, in April 2006, affected the world of hip hop, his family, fans and friends. It filled me with sadness too. What are your thoughts about the tragic event? To what extend did it affect your life and artistry?

"Proof's death affected me in a number of ways. He was more like family than just a friend, ya know. He and I went to the same mosque for prayers and stuff.

Besides we were friends long before there was a D12. Actually, he told me that he wanted me in this crew that he was tryin' to get started that would feature all the freshest, dopest, hottest rappers in the city but he didn't have a name for it yet. We lost contact for sometime and when I saw him again, he said, "You know you're supposed to be in the Dozens (D12), right?"

But that's old news, he was my brother, he called my father ABU (Which is what I call my Dad). He called my mother ma or mama. He called my girl "Mrs. Mu" and he was there when she died. We spent a lot of time around each other and he kept music fun for me, but when he passed.... The fun was gone ya know. I saw people that he called Fam (blood and otherwise) that never even met his kids or knew their names as if they were around him all the time but...I kinda lost it when they had his Funeral in a church and they knew he was not a Christian.

Anyways, enough of that, 'cause I could go on & on. Bottom Line...It hurt me to the point that a part of me died with him. The FUN PART of doing MUSIC!!! Like losing my MOJO ya Know!!"

6. What is your opinion about the current state of hip hop?
""CORNY" and "EASY" as hell. There is no skill involved whatsoever!"

7. From what I understand, you have some brand new musical projects going on...can you tell us a little bit about them?
"Yeah...we just finished The K.R.A.M mix tape For Journalist103 and we are finishing an album on Bilal Rossi AKA B GUTTA, and YES I have a few NEW projects of my own that I'm working on as well. A SOLO project set to rival "The FLOOD" and a mix of exclusive unreleased material by me and PROOF. Both CD's should be Bananas!"

8. Old school or new school—where goes your preference?
"Definitely old school."

9. What is your outlook on the Detroit scene? What are its assets and what could or should be improved?

"Number One: show Promoters need to start paying local talent for shows. They pay everyone else from out of town but refuse to pay their own.

Number Two: You might wanna rephrase the question 'cause I don't know if you are talking about the City in general or just musically?"

10. Which (underground or mainstream) artist(s) has earned your respect and why?

"It's a lot, but I'll just name a few:(Underground) GUILTY SIMPSON, PARADIME, JOURNALIST 103,PAPOOSE, KIKO,MYSELF LOL, to name a few. (Mainstream) Jay-Z, Scarface, Geto Boyz, Kool G Rap, Serious Jones, MOP, Lauren Hill etc…"

11. A few words about one of your collaborators, Journalist 103?

"Journ is not only a really good friend, but he's also a very talented poet and MC with something to say about the world as we know it and deserves a really good listening to."

12. According to you, what makes you appear as unique in the world of hip hop?

"To sum it up in a few words…I don't just rap about things 'cause I think it sounds cool, and then pretend to live like that. I actually live it and then rap about it!"

Blade Icewood

Blade Icewood aka Darnell Quincy Lyndsey used to represent Detroit's Streetlordz, a Dirty Glove Entertainment group in which girls are as tough as males in their way of rapping: a good illustration of it is the Mobb song.

Blade Icewood was also nicknamed *"The Great Lakes Ruler"*

Dark and rhythmic instrumentals characterize the group. In 2005, Blade, who was about to rise as Detroit's new hip hop star, was fatally shot over a long-term beef that opposed the East Side Cheddar Boys to the Streetlordz. The same beef had also caused the loss of East Side Cheddar Boys' member Wipeout.

Obie Trice

Obie Trice—"real name, no gimmicks". Real as one can get, Obie Trice emerged from his underground status in 2003. The artist's first official release was entitled *Cheers*. *Cheers* showed some real lyrical skills, but it was a little bit too much mentored by Eminem whose strong influence you could feel throughout the whole CD. Obie's second CD, *Second Rounds On Me* is one of Detroit's most beautiful pieces of black music. The astute choice of the instrumentals combined with some lyrical fluency allows us to call this CD a masterpiece.

Obie Trice, who was signed to Eminem's label, decided to depart in 2008, mainly because of the lack of exposure. The talented emcee is currently working on his third CD, *Bottoms Up*.

Obie Trice, who has been rapping since the early age of 14, was known in school for his excellent literary skills. Despite all, he broke up with school very early in order to rap. He was also involved into drug deals and became homeless for a while (before Bizarre introduced him to Eminem in 2001), because his mom wouldn't tolerate it and she kicked him out of her home.

Dogmatic aka Kevin Bailey

Dogmatic aka Kevin Bailey is an authentic emcee coming straight from the 313. Close friend to Deshaun Holton aka Big Proof, Dogmatic released the Promatic CD with Proof in 2002. Promatic is the combination of Proof+ Dogmatic. Both artists worked together on a hilarious video entitled Do What I Wanna Do, in which Proof and Dogmatic behave like misbehaved school boys.

Dogmatic released two mixtapes "8 Mile Chronicles" 1 and 2 that fully reflect the Detroit ghetto spirit. The latest to date was released on April the 10th, 2012. It involves many local talents such as Raw Collection, Swifty Mc Vay, Obie Trice, and many more.

The following exclusive interview I did with Dogmatic back in 2007 will reveal more about the brilliant artist.

Exclusive Dogmatic interview (with Isabelle Esling, 2007)

1. How did you get started as an emcee?
> "It all started with the LL Cool J "I'm Bad" LP that my brother let me hear."

2. Your first nickname used to be K-Stone. How and why did you change it to Dogmatic?
> "I was very young as K-Stone like 8th grade through high school, but as I got older I grew out of that name and image so I chose a name that suited me more as an adult and that would keep me relevant for the new millennium. The name Dogmatic came from my mom. It's what she called me and my dad for having so many girlfriends, so I made the switch."

3. When did you meet Proof and to what extent did he affect your musical style?
> "I met Proof in 1991 in a freestyle session over our boy an emcee B-def's house, when I heard his wacky style it definitely opened me up to something new."

4. Tell me a little bit about your "Promatic" album.
> "It was hot it was fun and definitely before its time; a real classic piece and some of Proof's best work."

5. What inspired you to create the "Do What I Wanna Do" video?
> "Well the song of course, plus Proof wanted to do something different and crazy, so when I saw the treatment for the video I had to shoot it. But really my first choice for our video was the song, "Live", but we were having too much fun to do that."

6. Define your style within a few words...
> "If you would have asked me this last year I probably would have said, "Street Gully", but now the answer is just true hip hop in its purest form."

7. What is your 8 Mile Chronicles CD all about?

"It was about getting all the shit I been through in Detroit and in the rap game off my chest."

8. Proof's death affected most of us. What are your thoughts on the tragic event that deprived us from a brilliant emcee?

"I will always be in pain from that tragedy that cheated us all. It set me back emotionally plus changed me morally, but matured me a whole lot. I really wish I could change it or had been there to stop it from happening, but I couldn't. I know he's watching though, and I will keep making him proud and let his voice be heard; help take care of his family and keep Promatic alive."

9. Tell me a little bit about the Sick Notes label.

"I started Sicknotes Ent. in 2000 with my nephew Witt and our friend Pep. Some of our production credits are Promatic, the virus, D12 world, Obie Trice, Proof's searching for Jerry Garcia, Bizarre's "Handy Cap Circus", "8 Mile Chronicles", and more recently my new mixtape CD the reality show. You've probably heard some of our tracks on VH1's the white rapper show and MTV's Big and Rob."

10. What are your thoughts about the local Detroit scene?

"We have all the talent; we just need more love."

11. What are your biggest musical influences?

"All the old Motown stuff and the classic hip hop like Run Dmc, LL Cool J, Rakim and Eric B, P.E., EPMD, NWA, B.D.P., Nas, 2PAC."

12. Which artist do you respect most and why?

"Nas for carrying on tradition in hip hop; Master P for showing us our value and how to get it; Dr.Dre for giving us a quality standard in hip hop production; Ice Cube for showing us how to go from gangsters to business men; 2PAC (Tupac) for his pro blackness and teaching us to love ourselves. Andre3000 (from Outkast) for being original and teaching the kids, and KRS ONE for educating us."

13. What are your musical projects for 2007?

"There's a lot in the works a Dogmatic LP, and a mix tape (the reality show), an of course a new Promatic LP, Promatic mixtape and DVD."

14. What accomplishment are you most proud of?

"I would have to say my 2nd K-stone LP 313. It really changed shit in the D. It's what started that saying 313 in Detroit and all over the world people using area codes to represent their city. Hands down, that's my greatest accomplishment yet in hip hop, starting the slang 313."

Other rappers such as Dice, are also notorious for their underground work on the Detroit scene. Pardon me for the ones I have forgotten.

I-Mac, rebaptized I-Dash

I-Mac, later rebaptized as I-Dash is a locally notorious group composed of three members, Alonzo "Zo" Morgan, Tim "Hash" Bell, and Ladale "Reag" Robinson.

Their most impressive work is probably the Ruthless Aggression mix tape that offers a wide panel of instrumentals of diverse influences. Very rough in its concept, it unleashes some specific Detroit atmosphere. Scurrilous in its concept, it is lyrically very rich. The three members released an album entitled *Letitbump* in 2008. Using a lot of electronic sounds, the artists' style is changing, with a greater mainstream appeal, maybe.

DJ Rick

DJ Rick is a Puerto Rican rapper from Detroit. He used to live in one of the most dangerous areas of Detroit and started rapping in 1996. He is known for his collaborations with Detroit's MC Skully, Da Hardheads, DJ Butter.

He can be considered rather as a 'party rapper'. However, his music combines the soft and spicy Latino flavor with the raw Detroit dimension. Sometimes nostalgic sounding, his music can also become very joyful.

Sleeper Cell Records artists

Senim Silla (Of Binary Star), Naaman Norris, *Malaki The Most Hi and* Dj Bet from the *Sleeper Cell Records* family.

Malaki The Most Hi is a former Big Proof collaborator. His music in itself is a lyrical assault. Malaki's music is more representative of some alternative hip hop.

Notorious producers and DJs

If Detroit hip hop can be considered as excellent and heartfelt music, it is also thanks to its wide range of very competent producers and DJ's.

Besides deceased legendary producer Jay Dilla, who keeps inspiring hot artist such as Guilty Simpson of the Almighty Dreadnaughtz and producer Black Milk, Denaun Porter aka Kon Artis is probably one of the hottest producers on the Detroit scene.

Denaun Porter has co produced several Eminem albums, he is behind the productions of very famous videos such as 50 Cent's Stunt 101 video. He has collaborated with hip-hop legend Xzibit and is now offering his own brand of beats, Mr. Porter beats.

DJ P Dog aka Odell Perry happens to be one of Detroit's most gifted DJ's. The man literally 'talks with his hands'. Detroiters call him "The Turntable Bully" because of his impressing skills.

DJ Graffiti, DJ Babe, DJ Lenn Swann and DJ DDT, DJ Butter and DJ Head (D12's former DJ) are also notorious on the local scene for their multiple collaborations, numerous mix tapes and their dedication to their hometown, DETROIT.

A D12 Photo Journey

Proof with Eminem

*Front row: (left to right): Van Carlisle aka Kuniva,
Marshall Mathers aka Eminem, Rufus Johnson aka Bizarre.
Back row (left to right): Ondre Moore aka Swifty Mc Vay,
Deshaun Holton aka Big Proof, Denaun Porter aka Kon Artis*

D12 and G-Unit

Swifty

King Gordy - Respect

Jermaine—Uncle Ill

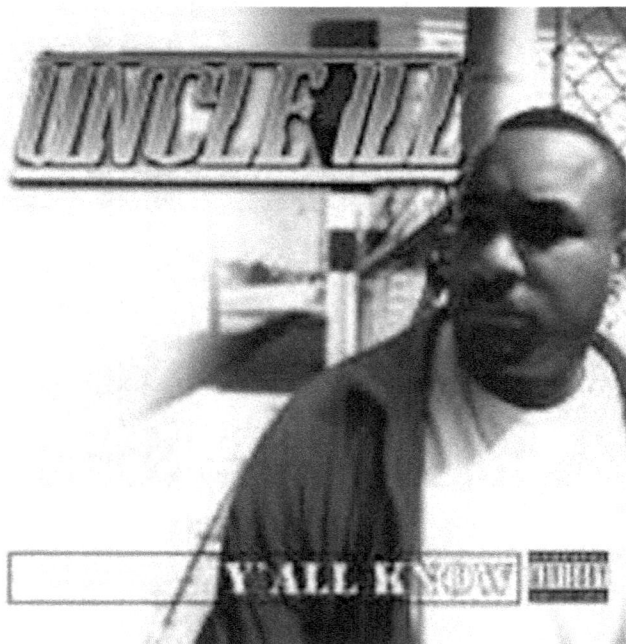

Uncle Ill

Kuniva

Promatic

Rufus Johnson aka Bizarre of D12

Kon Artis

Dogmatic

Proof & Dogmatic

Eminem with Barry Yett aka DJ Butter

Eminem with DJ Butter

Chapter 2

The Dirty Dozen—The Story Behind The D-12 Group

When being asked about D12, most people think about the six best known D12 emcees: Eminem, Proof, Bizarre, Swifty, Kuniva and Kon Artis.

But the story behind the D12 group is more complex than that and D12 used to have more emcees than the six names mentioned above.

In 1999, D12 lost a valuable emcee named Karnail Pitts aka Bugz. In 2006 the group lost its founder, Big Proof.

Long before that, there were two more emcees in the D12 group: MC Fuzz, (who can be heard in the Trife Thieves song out of Bizarre's *Attack Of The Weirdos*) in collaboration with Killa Hawk and Eye Kyu.

Killa Hawk, Eye Kyu and Fuzz left the group long before D12 could reach success.

A local Detroit emcee, Phat Cat aka Ronnie Cash once accused Eminem of stealing emcee Fuzz's rapping style. Eminem's response would follow in a rare live track called "Pick It UP", in which he addresses Phat Cat's comments directly.

If we take the D12 Underground EP as a reference, D12's musical style was very different from what it is now. The group used a lot of dark contrabass sounds mixed with some rhythmic piano notes. Musically, it was very close to jazz and soul sounds.

D12's deceased member Bugz possessed an incredible flow and some very inventive lyrical skills, as his These Streets EP shows. Bugz was probably one of Detroit's next raising stars, just after Eminem. Unfortunately, his young life was cut short at the early age of 21 over an argument at Belle Isle amusement park.

When Proof and Bizarre decided to create the D12 group, they had yet to define the group's goal. At first, D12 was supposed to be baptized "The Dirty Dozen", but the name of the group was changed to D12 as a jazz group in Detroit already carried the same name.

Proof founded D12 in 1995. It was Proof who introduced Eminem to Kon Artis, who didn't expect to see a white person at his door. *He was like' Hmm, what the fuck? White boy at my door!"* But within a month, they were all rhyming together, united by the same passion for rap music. Eminem was writing the rhymes and Kon Artis made the beats.

Kon Artis also produced Eminem's Infinite album.

According to Bizarre, Marshall's skin color wasn't much of an issue, as he was not the only white boy there living in a black neighborhood. Moreover, through his dedication to the music and his attitude, Eminem won his fellow members' heart. To the D12 member he isn't really *"white"* but rather the kind of white person with *"chocolate on the inside"*.

"That nigga ain't white. He got white in him, but he ain't white."

When the D12 crew uses the N word, it is, of course, deprived of any negative meaning. The original concept of D12 was to gather Detroit's 12 best emcees. Proof then decided that each of the group's six members would have an alter ego. Proof would become Derty Harry, Eminem Slim Shady, Bugz Robert Beck. Bizarre chose Peter S. Bizarre and his fellow emcee Kuniva went successively by 2 aliases, Hannz G and Rondell Beene. Denaun Porter became Kon Artis.

Before he died, Bugz always wanted his friend Ondre Moore aka Swifty Mc Vay to become a full member in D12, which happened after he died.

The tragic circumstances that surround Karnail Pitts death are revealed in a *Rolling Stone Magazine* article:

The day of the show, Bugz, a friend, and his friend's cousin were spending the afternoon at Detroit's Belle Isle Park. An altercation arose when a man sprayed Bugz' friend's cousin with a high-powered water gun and she took offence. A heated argument ensued which escalated into a fistfight, and Bugz intervened on his friend's behalf. At this point, a friend of the man with the water gun went into a Ford Expedition, drew a rifle, and fired at Bugz, who was looking away at the time. He was hit three times at close range, once in the neck, and once in the chest. The men then ran Bugz over in the Expedition. An ambulance was called, but due to traffic on the bridge to Belle Isle, it took them thirty minutes to get onto the island. Bugz was rushed to a nearby hospital, where he could not be saved. He had just turned twenty-one.

Bugz' death changed the D12 members' vision of life. It increased their determination to get started with their LP.

"It just makes you look at life more serious. At this point, we're trying to gather everything he recorded to make an LP." *(Proof)*

When Eminem inked with Dr. Dre's label, he temporarily interrupted his work with D12 with the idea to promote his group as soon as the occasion to do so knocked at the door—which happened in 2001.

The first member to become famous was supposed to show loyalty to the other members, which Eminem did straight away.

"Aside from everything, aside from all the bullshit, I know I've got a good heart. I know where my loyalty is. Pretty much all the guys in the group have told me that they never doubted me (coming back for them) because that was our pact from way back, from when we first started the group five years ago."

In the meantime, Proof carried on his work with his D12 fellows.

Devil's Night, D12's first mainstream album, totally reflects the spirit of the Detroit hood. Filled with a good dose of grime, a dark horror core effect, some foul mouthed and filthy lyrics, some heavy bass sounds combined with various instruments; Devil's Night took the world by storm.

In comparison with Devil's Night, D12 World (that was released in 2004), the group's second album was quite disappointing and had much more of a mainstream appeal.

Some songs, however, like How Come pointed the finger at some dissentions that began to part the group members; made them D12 emcees shine—Denaun Porter's vocals on How Come were admirable and very poignant.

During all the years that followed, the D12 emcees haven't stopped working on underground joints. The D12 online mix tape was relative to the beef that separated Benzino and Eminem, and on the local scene, Royce da 5.9 and Proof.

The tragic death of Deshaun Holton seemed to have put things on hold for a few months. But the D12 emcees would bounce back with The Return of the Dozen that excluded Eminem's participation.

Besides their common work within D12, most of the emcees have done some interesting solo work in their careers.

D12 Solo Work
Proof aka Derty Harry

> *I'm sure everybody who has ever met him, even just once, can testify to the fact that he illuminated a room when he walked in it. I believe that Proof loved people and people loved him. He was a magnet. He lured you in. You wanted to learn about him, follow his swagger. Without Proof, there would be no*

Eminem, no Slim Shady, and no D12. (Eminem's obituary speech at Proof's funeral)

Deshaun Holton aka Big Proof was born on October 2, 1973. Of all D12 emcees, Proof is probably the most prolific of all. His shiny personality and his huge connections with the Detroit scene allowed him to do some remarkable underground work. Deshaun Dupree Holton surely wasn't your "average Joe", in rap music. He was an extraordinary freestyler who managed to move crowds. He knew how to raise enthusiasm from his public, because he had this flame that very few hip-hop dedicated artists have for their art. Proof literally breathed hip-hop. He carried a dream that was bigger than him. It included the Detroit hip-hop scene as a whole. He wanted his hometown put on the map and united most fellow emcees to work together despite their differences. Nobody represented Detroit hip-hop better than Deshaun Holton. When Proof battled a rival, he'd kill his opponent verbally. Proof's lyrical bullets were feared on the local scene. His high respectability gave him the name "Living Proof" which meant "Living proof of hip hop".

Maurice Malone recalls a mic session in which Proof battled basketball player Chris Webber*:

I'll never forget when Chris Webber battled Proof. The Michigan basketball players would come by, and Chris came by one time after the famous game where he called time out and Michigan lost the championship against Duke. He goes on the mic, says what he says about Proof. Then Proof starts rapping and hits him with this line 'You don't have no time-outs'. Everybody starts laughing and Chris was so embarrassed. We were kind of pissed off at Proof 'cuz we never seen Chris again after that.

The Hip Hop Connection, December 2008

In 1996, Proof started emerging as an underground artist. One of his first releases was the *WEGO* mixtape in collaboration with Kevin Bell aka DJ Head. At the same time, his work with Detroit

pioneers 5 ELA (Thyme and Mudd), *Yester Years EP* came to frui-
tion. The same year Proof and Trick Trick released the *From Death
CD* in collaboration with Trick Trick's group *Da Goon Sqwad*.
Proof would also sit with Jay Dilla and both artists would release
a common song called Da Science.

The next year, Proof set his efforts on his common work with his
fellow D12 emcees *D12's Underground* EP.

In 1998, all D12 emcees put some tremendous work into Eminem's
Slim Shady EP.

Proof and his 5 ELA fellows gave light to several underground
jewels, The Album That Time Forgot and 5 ELA Pt3. Deshaun
Holton also actively participated to Bugz' underground masterpiece, These Streets EP, that is so much representative of the
Detroit ghetto.

The schedule of the 2000-2001 years kept Big Proof very busy,
especially with touring, as he officially became Eminem's hype man,
a role that is now held by Denaun Porter aka Kon Artis.

One can count Proof's talent as an essential element that insured
the "Devil Night" CD's success in 2001. While getting some mainstream recognition, Proof always kept true to the Detroit scene and
kept his work there very active.

The "Detroit What!" Mixtape was D12's underground release for
fall 2001.

Proof also collaborated with a long-time friend, Kevin Bailey
aka Dogmatic (formerly known as K-Stone) on their common
musical project Promatic, that combined both artists' names (
Proof+Dogmatic). This explosive, slang rhymed and hilarious
album was indeed the Promatic album.

The album included the witty "Do What I Wanna Do" video in
which both artists return to school for some perverted games.
Intentionally rebellious against their parents, both artists will make
you laugh from the beginning to the end.

But nobody will speak better about Promatic than Dogmatic himself:

> *It was hot, it was fun, and definitely before it's time a real classic piece and some of Proof's best work.*
>
> Exclusive Dogmatic interview, Isabelle Esling, 2007

Besides the Promatic album, Proof was also working on another musical project entitled *Electric Coolaid Acid* EP.

In 2004, Deshaun Holton released his excellent *I Miss the "Hip Hop Shop" mix tape* in which he offers the hip-hop listener a retrospective of the golden age of hip-hop. While Proof's nostalgic feelings about Maurice Malone's "Hip Hop Shop" resurface in a part of his brain, his CD is a constant demonstration of lyrical brilliance.

The "Grown Man Shit" mix tape, released in 2005, exposed a more mature Proof, who was now ready for reconciliation with his long-term enemies like the father of acid rap Esham. With his usual sense of humor and loads of wittiness some insignificant local haters are ridiculed and put in place by the free-styling master.

Deshaun Holton was known for his tenacity and his work in depth. After three years of hard work on his solo LP, 'Searching For Jerry Garcia' was eventually released on August 9, 2005.

The CD's release date was intentionally calculated in order to remember genius guitarist Jerry Garcia's 10th death anniversary. In his album, Proof also paid tribute to Kurt Cobain and Eric Clapton.

2005 also marked some interesting changes in Proof's career: the talented artist decided to create his own record label, Iron Fist Records, whose motto is and will remain: "IF to Death".

The Purple Gang group (First Born, Killa Kaunn, Flame and Famous), Woof Pac and Supa Emcee composed the Iron Fist music family. Proof was to be the CEO of the label.

In 2006, Deshaun Holton gathered a wide range of Detroit rap artist collaborations including his own Iron Fist label members and the "Hand To Hand" mix tape was born.

A few months before his death, Proof was working on an album that he completed within a record time of 24 hours. It is entitled *Time A Tell*, but it has yet to be released by Iron Fist officials.

When Proof died, a lot of tension would arise within the Iron Fist label. Darcey aka Rude, who happened to be the promotions director at Iron Fist, eventually left the label. In an interview we did together, Rude reveals his version of the story*:

> *I consider myself a loyal dude and I tried to hold on with the label as long as I could. At first it was just lil' stuff; people were getting in peoples ear starting stuff. Then it just got to the point where it was just not a label anymore. The office was turning into a playpen and no work was being done more and more groupie chicks started getting in peoples head blowing their heads up to the point to where they were turning their backs on what Proof left. He always said before every meeting "Ya'll are my kid's future. I'm investing in ya'll for my kids." The final straw was when disrespectful (1st born) jerks started coming at Proof's wife and not giving her any respect. Niggas (Killa Kaunn) started trying to sue her over money that was never theirs—just whack shit. Just got to the point where I was like I can represent Proof without the bullshit ya'll doing, so I dipped.*

Darcey aka Rude of *Iron Fist*
interview with Isabelle Esling, 2007

During his whole career, Proof has been collaborating with numerous local Detroit talents. Among them, the notorious Trick Trick and his Goon Sqwad, Jay Dilla, Hash, Purple Gang, Woof Pac, 5 ELA, Dogmatic, Royce Da 5.9, Slum Village, Malaki The Most Hi, Twiztid of Psychopatic Records and many more.

On a national scale, Proof also worked with numerous influential mainstream artists such as B Real of Cypress Hill, 50 Cent, Nate Dogg and Method Man.

Deshaun Holton's short life is the testimony of his true love for hip-hop. A love nobody can erase from the face of the earth.

Big Proof exclusive interview (January 2006)

I was very fortunate to be able to interview Deshaun Holton aka Big Proof in January 2006 thanks to Iron Fist's promotions director, just a few months before the brilliant artist got killed at the CCC club in 7 Mile, on April 11, 2006. I would like to share this exclusive interview with all of you.

Proof interview Q & A's

Deshaun Holton, aka Proof aka Derty Harry, thanks for accepting this interview.

1. Many people know you as the D12 member, but less people know you as a solo artist. Is that the main reason that motivated you to create Iron First?

"Yeah, it seems that the people forget the origin of D-12. All solo artists and whoever gets on, come back for the rest."

2. What is the main difference between the D12 artist and the solo artist you actually are?

"Basically, two different perspectives to speak from…"

3. In your "Searching For Jerry Garcia" album -tight album, by the way—suicide seems to be a recurrent theme…can you tell us a little bit more about your fascination with suicide and about "Club '27"?

"It's a metaphor, the death of Derty Harry, a cocoon state; it's a new beginning… "Club 27" is some spooky shit to me, a lot of incredible artists…"

4. Besides your love for your hometown that is present in your CDs and mixtapes, what or who is your main source of inspiration?

"Man life is the greatest inspiration, hands down."

5. D12 and Proof fans are familiar with your E.S.H.A.M. track and have followed your beef with local rapper Esham. On your "Grown Man Shit" mixtape, you apologize to him. I have heard that both of you have reconciled in Detroit at your birthday party. Do you have collaborations with Esham included in your future projects?

"Yeah, me and Esham gonna do some work very soon."

6. I miss "The Hip Hop Shop"; that beautiful mix tape of yours recalls the days of the Hip Hop shop in Detroit. Back in the day, what do you miss most about the early stages of Detroit hip hop?

"Wow! That's an ill question...I miss the innocence, the vibe and the adventure."

7. What is the most difficult challenge you had to face in your whole career?

"Separating the streets from the industry..."

8. Besides D12, you have much collaboration with local artists. Which Detroit artist (s) has (have) recently attracted your attention because of his (their) talent?

"Supa Mc, Woofpac, and J Hill. They all are very talented, and of course, Purple Gang."

9. Who are you keen on collaborating (whether on the local scene or on a national scale) with in a near future?

"Mike from Alien Ant Farm, he's a cool cat."

10. What kind of projects will you be working on after "Searching for Jerry Garcia?

"Hand to hand mix CD due out March 7th ... P.G. album, Woofpac, Supa M.C. then Club 27, we just started on the 3rd D-12 album...so be on the look out; we coming full steam ahead."

Rufus Johnson aka Bizarre

Rufus Johnson aka Bizarre was born on July 5, 1976, in Detroit. Very recognizable by his heavy weight shape and his shower cap; D12's member Bizarre is probably one of the most underrated emcees within the group.

His sick, hilarious lyrics that characterize him are not always to everybody's taste. Bizarre, however, has developed his own, original style since 1997 and made a name for himself on the local and international scene.

Bizarre earned his stage name because of a 5th grade teacher who noticed that little Rufus spent a lot of time talking to himself and rapping in class. That's how Rufus Johnson was called "Bizarre kid".

> *I was like 10 or so, in the 5th grade…I used to talk to myself and say raps to myself in the classroom and one day my teacher said I was a Bizarre Kid. I was just stuck.*

Bizarre's weirdness might not make unanimity among his critics. As a person, well…because of his originality, he might be perceived as very different from the average citizen:

> *I'm the type of guy that talks to bums, I don't avoid them. I ask them for money, before they can ask me…*

Bizarre's first underground album, "The Attack Of The Weirdos" (that is quite notorious on the local Detroit scene), was produced by Denaun Porter, Mc Hush, Jay Dilla and DJ Head. It had a lot of interesting collaborations such as DJ Head, DJ Lenn Swann, Mad Chemist and The Outsidaz. The album earned the "Inner City Flava of The Year" award in 1998. The same year, Bizarre focused on his Unreleased Demo 1998, an original and interesting piece of work.

Musically speaking, it would be quite difficult to categorize Bizarre. Highly influenced by KRS-One, Bizarre allies insanity with hilarity, which perfectly fits into the surreal atmosphere that emanates from his music. At a young age, Bizarre already showed some good rapping skills, battling older emceeing buddies.

> *My style is unorthodox and ill—been that way since day one. I always wanted to be different. When I was young, I was battling niggas twice my age.*

On a national scale, Bizarre has worked with a wide range of artists such as Redman, Tha Alkoholics and Method Man, just to name a few.

Inside of D 12, Bizarre is the weirdo of the group. In his ill rhymes, he can talk about anal sex and raping his grandma like a random person would lead to a normal conversation. Bizarre is there to shock you and to make you raise eyebrows.

Back in the days, Bizarre and Eminem enjoyed challenging themselves.

> *"I would pitch a lot of sick shit to my partner, Eminem, and we'd build off each other."(Bizarre)*

A beautiful example of Bizarre and Eminem's collaboration is the Amityville song from the Marshall Mathers LP. The duo is sick, insane, scary, in short the perfect lyrics to a horror core scenario that takes place in Detroit, the Murder Capital.

Besides his common work on D 12's CDs, Devil's Night and D 12 World, Bizarre released two solo CDs, Hanni Cap Circus and Blue Cheese and Coney Island.

2005 was the year Bizarre differentiated himself from his fellow D12 emcees. That's when he founded his own label, Read Head Records.

While Hanni Cap Circus puts the accent on Bizarre's eccentric personality Blue Cheese and Coney Island will allow the listener to understand Bizarre's various musical influences and how Detroit (his hometown) and Atlanta (the city he chose to relocate in) shaped his behavior.

Hanni Cap Circus presents "B12" as the D12 group's new rock star. It includes Eminem and Obie Trice's participation.

Blue Cheese and Coney Island is a very valuable CD that involves a range of gifted artists such as Detroit vocalist, Monica Blaire, King Gordy, Scarchild, Tech9ne and Detroit lyrical genius Young Miles.

Monica Blaire actually happens to be one of Detroit's best contemporary soul, R&B artists. She sings with heart and manages to touch her audience emotionally.

Besides his official LPs, Bizarre also has two new mix tapes: Bizarre's World and the latest to date, "Hate Music" in collaboration with King Gordy.

On February 28th, Bizarre officially announced his split from the D12 group:

> *It's a personal decision on my part. I think I've just grown as an artist and it's time for me to branch off on my brand," Rufus Johnson aka Bizarre.*

Undeniably, there were some artistic dissentions within the D12 group and Rufus Johnson, who felt differently about his music, decided to part ways with his former friends and collaborators.

His last up to date CD is entitled "This Guy's A Weirdo". It dropped on March 30, 2012. In this brand new mixtape, the Detroit artist advocates originality and "weirdness":

> *It's just encouraging people that it's alright to be weird, it's alright to be different and speak your mind and dress and look however the f**k you wanna look. It's a weirdo movement; it's time for that. Hip Hop is changing anyway, it's getting more and more outrageous how they looking.*

Ondre Moore aka Swifty Mc Vay, the lyrical bomber in D12

Detroit native Ondre Moore was born on May 16, 1976. The talented emcee chose his nickname after Oklahoma bomber Timothy Mc Veigh. The terrorist inspired him because of his attitude.

> *I'm not saying what he did to Oklahoma was all good, but it's just like, seeing him on TV, he was so nonchalant about it. Quiet, straight-faced, up-front, didn't have nothin' to hide. While pop-psych observations should be taken with a grain of salt, there's more than a little resonance here with another*

> *close-cropped white guy who stared down a nation of critics*
> *and accusers and said, simply, "What!"*
>
> Swifty Mc Vay

The correlation between Timothy Mc Veigh and Swifty Mc Vay is intentionally well-chosen. The difference between both men is that Swifty drops his bombs on the mic, causing lyrical carnage.

Be ready to get smashed by his avalanche of words.

The spelling of his stage name varies; so don't be surprised to find Swifty's name spelled as Swift, Swifty, Swifty Mc Vay and finally Swifty Mc Veigh.

Swifty first belonged to the Da Rabeez group before he belonged to D12. Accordingly to Bugz' wish, Swifty became a full member of D12 after Bugz unexpectedly died in May 1999.

Among his five other partners in crime, Swifty's interest for terrorism distinguishes him from his group. Discover some of his "criminal rhymes" taken out of D12's underground song "Shit On You":

> *"I remain fatter than gluttony*
> *Tapin' bombs on the back of record companies (uh huh)*
> *blow 'em up if they ain't wantin' me*
> *The national guard—they scared of huntin' me*
> *I love beef—I got your hoe duckin' me*
> *A drug thief—Bitch I'll take your marijuana*
> *These slugs will keep your ass away from my corner*
> *I drown niggaz in hundred degree saunas*
> *You can act a fool if you wanna—BIATCH*
> *It's this lyrical piranha—strapped with a grenade in a pool*
> *with yo' mama*
> *attack her by the legs and pull her to the bottom*
> *Twit lettin' up like a condom*
> *Slappin' if you fuckas got a problem*
> *When I see 'em—you hoes endin' up in a fuckin' mausoleum*
> *or hidden in a trunk of a black and gold BM*
> *Pull in a garage while you screamin'*

keep the motor on and I'm leavin'
I'LL SHIT ON YOU…"

Matter of fact, Swifty knows how to handle words. There are pretty good examples of his lyrical assault, like the Instigator song on D12's Devil's Night album.

In 2002, Swifty Mc Vay founded his own label, Da Fyre Department that employs a bunch of gifted Detroit native emcees.

If you dig deeper into Swifty's underground work, you'll find some masterpieces like the Grenade Pins and Forest Fyres mixtape.

In 2009, Swifty released two volumes of his Underestimated mixtape that can be defined as pure fire. His lyrical craft is astonishing.

Denaun Porter aka Kon Artis

Denaun Porter was literally born into the music. His father belonged to a famous gospel group, "The Five Blind Boys of Alabama". When Denaun's mom became pregnant, Mr. Porter Senior would stop his musical activities in order to raise his family. Sometimes, when parents are unable to pursue their dreams, kids will go ahead and carry their parents' dream, like Denaun did for his dad:

When I was in my mama's stomach, my dad stopped his career to come and raise me. So I'm taking the torch from my dad because he didn't get to spread the wings the way he wanted to, but he can spread his wings through me.

His participation to the Runyon Ave mixtape, some D12 underground work that is less known to the public, also reveals the rapper's competence. The Kuniva—Bizarre duo on Eminem's Re-Up mixtape, "Murder", is written in a dark, rough style with some heavy instrumentals. The track fully reflects the spirit of the Detroit hood.

Another CD that reveals Kuniva's lyrical craft is D12's underground mixtape; The Return of the Dozen, which came out in 2008. Less known from the mainstream public, Kuniva's underground work fully deserves an attentive exploration. His recent releases, "Feeling the Rush", "Hard As Mine" and "Bad Intentions" totally enlighten the artist's solo effort. The sharpness of his lyrics, the originality of his instrumentals will raise some attention from hip-hop loving ears.

Sadly for the D12 group, Denaun Porter, who became officially Eminem's hype man in 2009, announced that he had left D12 through twitter on March 24, 2012 because his aim was now to concentrate on his solo career.

Denaun Porter is planning to release his solo album, "The Memo", current 2012. Mr. Porter explained that his decision was not against the group. In a series of recent tweets, Mr. Porter showed respect and love to his former crew:

> *I love every moment I have shared on this planet and with the people I shared it with I will always love the legacy I was a part of. I got nothing but love for my crew I am growing and excelling, as u should as an artist. I hope you all support that.*

> *I want nothing but the best for @McVayD12 @kuniva and @Bizarresworld what proof created was beautiful and we had a great ride! Love N light.*

Denaun Porter also announced, among other details, the annihilation of the "Kon Artis" character.

Chapter 3

Eminem's Artistic Evolution Within A Decade

Going through life's hardships shaped Marshall Mathers and helped him gain maturity, personally and artistically. The artist transformed pains, sorrows and grieving into some admirable and meaningful songs.

All through the years, Eminem's musical work has been very complex. It mixes verbal dexterity, sarcasm, real emotions, self-hatred, hopes, joy and sorrows together. Within a decade, the direction Eminem gave his music changed a lot. From the pissed off and frustrated, broke emcee on the Slim Shady LP to the multimillionaire artist who recognizes publicly his addiction problem on his "Relapse" CD, and eventually showing the way out of a long tunnel of addiction in his seventh "Recovery" album. Eminem's inspiration opened the gates to new musical experiments.

His comeback, in 2009, was based on facing his addiction battle. As the artist states it in a 2011 *New York Times* interview lead by journalist Deborah Solomon,

> *Battling addiction in rehab-and out of rehab—wasn't really easy... The first time I went it was in Brighton, Michigan. The second time I didn't go to rehab. I just went to a regular hospital. I detoxed in the hospital, and then I came home. I couldn't go back to rehab. I felt like I was Bugs Bunny in rehab.*

> *When Bugs Bunny walks into rehab, people are going to turn and look. People at rehab were stealing my hats and pens and notebooks and asking for autographs. I couldn't concentrate on my problem.*

Marshall Mathers differs from many other emcees.

To understand his music, you really have to understand his life story, because each Eminem CD is fulfilled with very personal references and details. To a certain extent, Eminem allows his fans and listeners to become a little bit nosey about his privacy.

Family members, work place, enemies, dates and memorable events, everything is listed in his songs, in order to allow some insight from the fans' view.

Of course, Eminem's intention to share his life story like a live show has been largely misinterpreted by some obsessive people who are unable to keep a respectful distance towards the artist's privacy.

Never mind. There will always be "Stans", I guess.

Marshall's way to the top

A young man named Marshall Mathers dropped out of school after failing his grade three times. Failing at school wasn't due to a lack of intelligence, but rather to a lack of interest. Also, when you are getting bullied at school every single day, you are busy thinking about staying alive versus focusing on school subjects. *I don't think it was necessarily because I am stupid. I didn't go to school, I couldn't deal.*

With the humor that is so characteristic to most of his songs, Eminem recalls these awful high school times:

> *In school I never said much, too busy having a head rush*
> *Doing too much rush/ had my face flushed like red blush*

> Eminem, "I Just Don't Give A Fuck" song

After leaving school, Marshall Mathers was dealing with a double fight: finding a job and trying to become a rapper.

He eventually found a job at Gilbert's Lodge where he worked for a minimum wage salary ($5.50 per hour). Marshall used to work there with his former high school friend Mike Ruby.

Mike Ruby was also Marshall's rapping partner. Both, Mike and Marshall, used to record songs in Mike Ruby's basement. While Mike went by the stage name Manix, Marshall chose M&M (from his initials), which would later become Eminem. Both buddies' label was called " Bassmint Productions" where Marshall recorded a song titled, "Crackers 'N Cheese".

Despite his numerous attempts to get a chance to rap in places like Mike's basement, Eminem would soon notice that his skin color appeared to be more than an issue to many people.

Fellow white emcee Shortcut eventually introduced Eminem to local African American rapper Champtown:

> *Back then he (Em) never had a hook to a song. It would be like he was just telling a story. He never had hooks. Champ was one of the people who brought him in and showed him things, showed him hooks and humor.*

Shortcut, Metro Times, 2010

The collaborations with Champtown would eventually lead to an open door to the black hip-hop scene for Eminem who also attended freestyle sessions with his best friend Proof at the Hip Hop Shop during the same period, at Proof's initiative.

The Hip Hop shop eventually gave the aspiring rapper a sense of belonging to a community and the feeling it was accepted because of his skills:

> *The Hip Hop Shop was the heart of Detroit and it was definitely a place to come to show your skills. But it was emcees who were 'like' fuck the bullshit; we don't care what color you are, just rap. If you can rap, you've got a place with us. So basically, that's where I felt at home. The first time I rapped,*

> *I got warm reception, then it became like an addiction, every week just going there and freestyling. And I had never lost a freestyling battle in Detroit so that was a big thing too.*
>
> Eminem

In the world of freestyle battles, acceptance is everything. Lyrical brilliance and a good dose of wickedness that makes your rival fail are expected from the audience. The more battles you win, the bigger you become on the local scene.

Eminem's first big challenge was to battle an emcee named Kuniva (now a full D12 member) in order to prove his credibility. In the end, people were looking forward for him to spit his brilliant rhymes on stage.

The concept of a shock rapper

Two local Detroit producers, Jeff and Marky Bass were quite impressed with Marshall Mathers when they first heard him free-style, at the age of 15. He was only a teenager, but he was capable of handling complex syllabic rhymes, which would leave the Bass brothers in awe:

> *He was amazing at that age. He combined a lot of triple-tongue stuff with some best rhyming I'd ever heard. He was incredible.*
>
> Marky Bass

Marky Bass became one of the producers for his debut album "The Slim Shady" LP.

Despite the hard work and Eminem's obvious lyrical brilliance, both producers intuitively figured out there was something essential missing in the artist's music that could bring him to the top.

Marky and Jeff eventually invented the concept of a *shock rapper.*

> *We stayed in the studio every day for five years. We worked hard on getting him to the point where he is now; there was*

a lot of grooming and a lot of technique. We didn't want to throw Em out as just another rapper.

We came out with the idea of shock rap. When we went to Interscope (Eminem's parent record company), we worked with him as the Marilyn Manson of rap. Marshall was about 24 at this time. Things were going a little berserk in his life; labels that didn't want a white rapper were turning us away. We said, 'you've got to let this out and ride with it.'

His early stuff was accepted within the rap genre and by the critics, he was always clean with his lyrics and his delivery, but the market didn't take to it until it got a little foul-mouthed, a little potty-mouthed. Now, they'll take anything from the kid.

Marky Bass
www.geocities.com/angryblonde/159/articlesaustralia2002

This concept *has* proven to be successful.

No matter how good an artist might be at doing his thing and regardless of his high level of skills, you got to consider a CD from an entrepreneurial point of view: the CD is a product that needs to be marketed.

In terms of good marketing, a good evaluation of your target audience, and their needs (what they actually expect to hear from you) are mandatory.

With the unexpected and tragic death of his best friend and Uncle Ronnie in 1991, Marshall interrupted his work on rap music for four years. His daughter Hailie's birth acted like the detonator that would bring him back to his passion.

Back to rap in 1995, Eminem became part of several groups like "*New Jacks*" and "*Soul Intent*" who released his first single, "Biterphobia", a song that totally reveals Eminem's lyrical brilliance back in the day.

The same year, Proof founded D 12 along with fellow emcee Bizarre.

Due to some personal and financial problems, Eminem was forced to stop rapping for a six-month period. At this time, he was doing overtime (60 hours a week) at a restaurant in order to support his family.

In 1996, the "Infinite" album came out. Eminem and many of his collaborators had set a lot of hope on "Infinite"; it was intelligently worded and positively oriented. In his album, Eminem rapped about unity, love and moving ahead, even in hard times.

"Infinite" was really good and lyrical. But one of the album's main defaults was the lack of technical means, particularly if you consider the way the instrumentals sounded on the CD. Moreover, Eminem reminded people of Jay—Z and Nas.

The public's reactions towards the album and the lack of sales showed that Eminem had yet to find his real identity.

At this time, the emcee was really discouraged. He now envisions Infinite as a demo, as it was representative of what his style should be in the future:

> *"Infinite" was me trying to figure out how I wanted my rap style to be, how I wanted to sound on the mic and present myself, it was a growing stage. I felt like "Infinite" was like a demo that I just got pressed up.*

Marc Kempf, who was responsible for Eminem's management before Paul Rosenberg recalls Eminem's brilliant use of the English language:

> *Rather than rhyme the last syllable, Eminem will rhyme that last six syllables…his mastery of the English language allows him to write coherent stories, not just load off freestyle ramblings that happen to rhyme.*

The birth of Slim Shady

Slim Shady, Eminem's evil alter ego, has made history in rap music, stalking the earth for as long as there would be rap fans. But there is an interesting story behind the creation and the concept of Slim Shady.

The concept of an evil alter ego emerged in Eminem's mind after a trip to New Jersey with his friend Rufus Johnson aka Bizarre and The Outsidaz.

After having a closer look at Eminem's music, Bizarre insisted on the fact his music needed to sound grimier. The existence of an evil alter ego would, of course, set up more wickedness in his music. Since each D12 member needed an alter ego, Eminem needed to find his too.

Slim Shady popped into Marshall's mind at a rather unexpected place. While sitting in the bathroom, the name of Slim Shady suddenly emerged from his mind. Slim Shady is supposed to represent all the forbidden and hidden thoughts the artist has in mind:

> *I was taking a dump on the toilet, I swear to God. And that name just came to me-Slim Shady! It made sense right away, and I immediately thought about 20 million things that rhymed with it. So I wiped my ass, got off the pot and went and called everybody I knew.*

In 1997, Eminem's second underground album, The Slim Shady EP was in preparation. Contrasting with his first release, Infinite, the Slim Shady EP was written in a total different spirit.

Eminem's mind would suddenly slide into two parts: the regular guy and the monster, Dr. Jekill and Mr. Hyde. Slim Shady is Mr. Hyde in all his horrific dimension: he's the chainsaw murderer, the serial killer, the woman hater, and the rapist. Slim Shady the psychopath will take revenge from the world's rejection and spread his venom worldwide. The sudden outpouring rage that comes out of Slim Shady's mouth will cause a lot of astonishment, applause and controversy from people.

Schizophrenic delirium condensed in a verbal tornado, that's probably what summarizes the Slim Shady character quite well. Of course, the Slim Shady character requires a sense for a second thought from the auditorium. If you are missing the artist's dark sense of humor, you'll probably take him for a mad man.

"I had this whole Slim Shady concept of being two different people, having two different sides of me. One of them was trying to let go, and I looked at the mirror and smashed it. That was the whole intro of the Slim Shady EP. Slim Shady was coming to haunt me.

Slim Shady is just the evil thoughts that come into my head. Things I shouldn't be thinking about. Not to be gimmicky, but people should be able to determine when I am serious and when I'm fucking around. I got a warped sense of humor I guess."

Controversy constantly fuelled Eminem's career, since a lot of people misinterpreted and misquoted him. However, the controversy also happened to be an incredible promotional tool that greatly contributed to high CD sales.

Take each single word in Eminem's CD literally, you'll get offended. Fortunately, most people who are appreciative of his music are intelligent enough to realize when the artist is joking or not.

> *My true feelings were coming out, and I just needed an outlet to dump then in. I needed some type of persona. I needed an excuse to let go of all this rage, this dark humor, the pain, and the happiness. I don't need therapy. Every single word I say doesn't necessarily mean something. (Eminem)*

Like Paul Rosenberg, Eminem's manager pointed it out in July 2010 on the SOHH.Com website, Eminem anticipates reactions from people he is dissing in his records. Being a big attention seeker, he wants a reaction:

> *He gets a real kick out of getting a rise out of people--he wants a reaction. Whether you hate it, love it or think it's hilarious. It's like he's throwing the paper airplane in class to see who*

is paying attention--that's how his mind works. It's not as if he enjoys taunting, but he does like poking people, pushing their buttons. At the same time, this is a grown-up version of Eminem, but not Adult Contemporary by any stretch. It's an evolved person, who's evolving musically as well. (Paul Rosenberg)

The complexity of Eminem's rhymes often leads to the greatest misunderstandings and the creepiest behaviors. It is precisely the misinterpretation of his words Eminem is warning people against.

While the average fan might not be attentive to it, the connoisseurs' ears will catch his verbal constructions and punch lines with delight.

In 1997, Eminem was dealing with a lot of personal and financial problems. The situation got so bad that he was literally unable to pay his bills:

I'll never forget this. I was staying in the house with no heat—all the electric was cut off and everything. I was so mad-literally, like so emotional-I almost felt like cryin.'

Things even worsened to the point that Marshall got evicted from his home. The only choice left was to move into his mother's home where he wrote the first song to his "Slim Shady EP"; "I Just Don't Give A Fuck". During this period, as shown in the video to, "I Just Don't Give A Fuck" Eminem got hooked on drugs and alcohol.

In addition to all this, Kim would also forbid Marshall to see his daughter. When she finally accepted, Marshall used his daughter's voice in the '97 "Bonnie And Clyde" song.

Rapping about killing his baby's mother and dropping her into the lake with his little baby daughter as his main accomplice, Eminem shocked a lot of narrow-minded people. The song epitomized domestic violence.

In fact '97 "Bonnie and Clyde" is nothing else but the expression of a deep frustration in his love life. A lover takes his revenge and his trying to conquer his sweetheart again. Eminem has never been the kind of romantic dreamer, so the listener has to read the song between the lines in order to understand the hidden meaning behind the words.

Eminem also wanted to share his emotions and frustrations with his listeners and invite them into his world.

Catapult to the top

> *"Look, if you had one shot, or one opportunity*
> *To seize everything you wanted in one moment*
> *Would you capture it or just let it slip?"*
>
> Eminem, "Lose Yourself"

The *Slim Shady EP* marked a decisive step in Eminem's beginning career. Thanks to its original concept, a high level of lyrical competence and some interesting narrative skills, Eminem suddenly raised some interest from the media. This is how Eminem got featured in the Source magazine and portrayed as *the "crème de la crème emcee"* by an enthusiastic hip hop magazine owner and underground rapper named Benzino.

In a desperate publicity stunt to sell his music, Ray Benzino would pull out the race card against Eminem in 2003.

Just after his suicide attempt, in 1997, an interesting opportunity would knock at Eminem's door: Wendy Day, the founder of "Rap Coalition" invited Eminem to enter a rap contest. Marshall Mathers felt like he had nothing to lose, and accepted immediately. He would just grab the chance destiny seemed to offer him. There was a $500 prize to win. Unfortunately, Eminem ended second, just after an emcee called MC Juice. Discouraged, because he really expected to be placed in pole position, Eminem felt depressed. Nothing seemed really important from then on. The talented emcee didn't' really pay attention to the fact Jimmy Iovine from Interscope was asking for a demo tape. "Yeah, just take it", he would answer.

Eminem didn't really guess the enormous impact this event would have on his destiny. Jimmy Iovine played the tape to the notorious Dr. Dre.

Dr. Dre and Eminem

Andre Young aka Dr. Dre, the hip hop mogul, was used to listening to demos all the time. Usually, he didn't find anything really worth his interest. But it was different this time. Dr Dre liked Eminem's work instantly and he wanted to meet him.

To Eminem all this was a little bit of a fairy tale and kind of surrealistic. He'd been a fan of Dre and NWA for all those years and now he'd talk to his idol face to face! He was truly living up a fantastic dream.

The funny side of the story is that Andre expected Marshall to be black. Kind of surprised to discover that the young man was white, he nevertheless believed in his talent:

> *You know, he's got blue eyes, he's a white kid. But I don't care if he's purple. If you can kick it, I'm working with you.*

> Dr. Dre

Like many people who know that they are at a crucial turn in their lives, Eminem was feeling nervous at the beginning. But soon he'd feel the chemistry between him and Andre, the kind of chemistry that makes real friendships work.

"It was a dream come true to me. I had to shake the butterflies at first. But it was also anxiousness to just go there and show him what I could do. Ever since the first day we got into the studio, I knew we had chemistry."

Today Eminem and Dr. Dre are long time friends. *"Dr. Dre saved my life,"* says Eminem.

Eminem's first mainstream album, the Slim Shady LP was released on February 23rd, 1999 and made triple platinum. "My Name Is", Eminem's introduction to the world became a major hit.

Good events never come alone: on June 14th, 1999, Eminem tied the knot with Kim.

Dealing with the disadvantages of fame

Anybody who struggles for recognition has a representation of what the future might look like, after achieving one's goal. Most people would be longing for financial stability and recognition from the world. Eminem did too, but he really didn't expect to face the reverse of the medal:

> *First I thought I wanted the fame, the personification of polite, attentive interviewee today, I wanted a better life. But then all the kids screaming. All the girls falling at my feet. It came so fast that I didn't know what hit me. And it turned out that it wasn't even what I was looking for.*

Eminem probably wasn't prepared for such a busy schedule either. It was like he lost control of time:

> *Sometimes, I feel like I am living my life for someone else. I wake up at 7 in the morning and the rest of the day is work. I can't sleep. I don't eat. It's just crazy.*

So be careful what you wish for, Eminem warns his audience in his *Relapse* Bonus track:

> *So be careful what you wish for*
> *Cause you just might get it*
> *And if you get it then you just might not know*
> *What to do with it cause it might just come back on you 10 fold!*
>
> Eminem, "Be Careful What You Wish For,"
> Relapse Bonus track

Not only is it lonely at the top, but also coming out of nowhere, a bunch of crazed individuals claiming to be your fans invade your privacy, acting in the most disrespectful way one could imagine.

Because of his personal approach in his songs, some fans probably thought it allowed them to come closer to the artist in real life.

Some fans also come from the point that the artist owes them something, because they are buying his records.

An artist is just a professional doing his job. Your knowledge of an artist's biography and his CDs doesn't allow you to force yourself into his life like an unwanted intruder.

When Eminem bought his house in Sterling Heights, people would just violate the property and use the swimming pool:

> *I get motherfuckers coming to my house, knocking on the door.*
> *Either they want autographs or they want to fight.*

Eminem's major hit from the *Marshall Mathers* LP "Stan" warns obsessed fans against extreme behaviors. The explosion of the Internet increased the phenomenon of mad online stalkers, though.

So what is the difference between a big fan and a mad stalker?

An intelligent approach of the artist and his music makes all the difference. The big fan can make a difference between fiction and reality. Unlike the many "Stans", he usually possesses a good common sense that allows him to take a reasonable and respectful distance from the artist. The normal fan isn't deprived of his sense of criticism towards the artist, no matter what the artist says.

He told ya'll: he's just a regular guy. What more do you want from him?

Controversy and acclaim

Lyrics, lyrics constant controversy"
"Now this looks like a job for me
so everybody just follow me
'cause we need a little controversy
'cause it feels so empty without me

Eminem, "Without Me"

Whether people like it or not, controversy is the element that helps to capture a maximum of attention and sell a product. Internet users and forum owners perfectly know that forums with daily drama and arguments are the most successful. In the same way, controversy around the *Marshall Mathers* LP largely increased its sales.

While the *Slim Shady* LP enhanced Eminem's rhyming ability and brought some shocking stories to the world, the *Marshall Mathers* LP sparked more controversy. The lyrical masterpiece came out on May 23, 2000.

Because of his use of *'misogynistic and gay bashing sounding lyrics'*, *Eminem* became GLAAD's main target (Gay and Lesbian Alliance Against Defamation)

GLAAD Executive Director, Joan M. Garry said about Eminem's lyrics:

Eminem's hate-filled lyrics have not only brought many people together in opposition, they've also raised the issue of corporate responsibility for the marketing of this kind of product.

Eminem likes to shock people. Does he really mean what he states in his songs? The main mistake people make about Eminem is often due to their lack of knowledge of hip-hop culture. In fact,

Eminem is not the only rapper to use words such as "faggot", "bitch", "slut" and other similar cusswords. A lot of rappers did it before him and some still do.

Ice Cube's lyrics, for instance, are as offensive as Eminem's.

People seem to forget that rap music is ghetto music. Ghetto music goes with cusswords. The common meaning of "faggot" is "sissy".

The worst thing that could happen to a man in the ghetto is to be perceived as a coward. One mustn't forget that one of the main rules in rap music—besides lyrical fluency and stormy flow delivery—is disrespecting your rival. Negative critics often don't have a clue about the rules of rap music, that's why pointing a finger against "misogynist rappers" is meaningless as well. If it is true that rappers will disrespect "hoes" and " bitches"; female rappers will even come harder at males in their songs.

Real rap music is rebellious and rough in its essence as it reflects life in the hood. Why blame the messenger for telling things the way they are?

Eminem has often been described as a hate monger, a very bad influence for high school kids, and an example for the American society's decay. Eminem is not the danger, but the literal interpretation of his lyrics and the total misunderstanding of his warped sense of humor is. That's why parental supervision can help kids understand the artist's music better, which implies more open mindedness from the parents, of course, and an acceptance of their kids' musical tastes.

2001 was the year of the *Devil's Night* CD release. Eminem was now ready to introduce his D12 fellows and collaborators to the world.

The release of Marshall Mathers' semi-autobiographical movie, "8 Mile", in November 2002, eventually allowed the mainstream public to get to know Eminem better. Thanks to "8 Mile" the non hip hop initiated could understand the context that made Eminem and where he came from.

Eminem would use his new gained maturity and a sharp sense of criticism towards the Bush administration in his third mainstream album, *The Eminem Show*.

The originality of *The Eminem Show* is the depth of its political and social commentary of contemporary America. At the same time, Marshall Mathers reminded the attentive listener that he was part of black America. *The Eminem Show* also added some personal details that allowed the fan to follow his life story like he would follow a live TV show.

While still controversial, *The Eminem Show* granted Marshall more approval from a various audiences.

While his fourth CD, *Encore*, released on November 16, 2004, seemed to show some artistic fatigue, it still contained some good lyrical and politically engaged songs like "Mosh". New autobiographical details were added in "Evil Deeds" and Eminem had to defend himself against accusation of racism from *The Source* co-owner Benzino in "Yellow Brick Road", where he recalls the passion for rapping he shared in his high school days with Proof.

Has Eminem foreseen the death of his best friend? A flashback at the events that happened on April 11, 2006 at the infamous CCC club might allow us to think so.

In "Like Toy Soldiers", Eminem envisions Proof's fictional murder to set an example against violence and rivalry in hip hop. The video, that features Detroit's local underground rapper Mu, pictures a lyrical battle that involves Detroit emcees and 50 Cent's clan against Benzino and Murder Inc's crew that turns ugly. Proof loses his life and leaves Eminem devastated.

A retrospective look at the video will give most rap fans the chills.

Facing a lot of personal and health problems in 2005 that forced him to cancel his European tour, Eminem retired from the scene.

The death of his best friend on April 11, 2006, and his short lived marriage to Kim that led to a divorce just a few days earlier, pushed Eminem into a deep depression.

He was hospitalized, but his hospitalization was just the beginning to a long road of recovery. Marshall Mathers' addiction to pills just increased over the years, because his intake of pills was his way of dealing with painful situations.

After a four-year musical hiatus, Eminem surprised his public by his sudden return, in May 2009, with the release of a brand new album, *Relapse*.

Fans learned from Marshall's mouth that he nearly died from an overdose of methadone on December 2007.*

Relapse is Eminem's public confession about his addiction problems. It is certainly one of his most complex albums. Commercial songs like "We Made You" and "Crack A Bottle", Eminem showed his astonished public that he hasn't lost one ounce of his lyrical skills.

The album is deep and requires an in depth listen. Otherwise, you might miss the main point. Dark themes like pill addiction, rape, and child abuse are mentioned in the album. Debbie Mathers appears again in "My Mom", but as the rapper stated it in a *Vibe* magazine interview, he was open for a further reconciliation with his estranged mom, as he realizes their common story of addiction.

Globally speaking, Eminem's artistic evolution, no matter what album is your preference; Marshall Mathers is a mastermind, with a subtle way of thinking. His astute combinations of syllables make a true genius of him. All through the years, he developed some very valuable narrative skills and improved his use of various instrumentals and beats.

Loathe him or love him, Dr. Dre's former pupil is now an uncontested authority in rap music.

> *It's no secret I had a drug problem. I just don't think my fans knew how bad it was. When I went to rehab in 2005 I went*

in for a sleep problem, or I guess a sleep problem is what I thought it was. But it was a drug problem and I wasn't ready to admit it. I was taking Valium, Ambien, and Vicodin. And I was taking a lot. If I was to give you a number of Vicodin I would actually take in a day? Anywhere between 10 to 20. Valium, Ambien, the numbers got so high I don't even know what I was taking. I barely made it through that Anger Management 3 tour [Summer 2005]. I got by on the skin of my teeth. I had a rehab doctor that was seeing me through to where I could just take enough to not get sick and be able to sleep at night. The whole idea was, get me through the tour, through these last couple of weeks, and then I'll check myself in.

When I went into rehab everyone else was ready for me to go, but I wasn't. Rehab was a really bad experience for me. Just being a celebrity and shit, I felt like a fish out of water. It was like, I don't have a problem. Everybody else has a problem. I'm a grown man. I should be able to do what I wanna do. That's the thing that addicts go through in their mind. I stayed in rehab for probably two weeks—then I checked myself out.

Needless to say, I relapsed. I started taking Vicodin the week after I got home, so I was probably clean for three weeks. Then I started back with the Nyquil. I had a problem with Nyquil even though it's an over-the-counter thing; it's a serious trigger for me. I'd try to knock myself out but sometimes if you drink too much it would have the reverse effect and keep you up. So I'm right back on the phone with the dopeman trying to get Valium or whatever I could to sleep. The problem was bad already, but when the Proof thing happened, it got really bad.

It's not an excuse to use drugs, but man, if I ever had a reason.... It was an excuse for me to just say, Fuck it. I just went all out with it. It got worse and worse to the point where I was getting it from anywhere I could. I had friends—or so-called friends—that were using the same shit that I was. They'd give me shit and I'd stockpile it.

So one day, this was right before Christmas of 2007, I got a hold of some pills. Somebody gave me some pills that were blue and they were shaped like Vicodin. I went to him looking for anything with codeine in it—Tylenol 3s, 4s, but they gave me these blue pills. They told me, take these, these are just like Vicodin, only they're easier on your liver. I remember taking one in the car on the way home, and I was like, Whoa, this is fuckin' great. I didn't even ask what it was. I'm like, this makes you mellow and it's easier on your liver? I got a new drug of choice.

Within a day or two I was back askin' for more. This time I probably got 15 to 20 of 'em. I think that day I took half. Toward the evening, I remember not being able to get out of bed. I literally couldn't move. People said that I was actin' weird that day—actin' real slow and shit.

I think I slept from 3 in the afternoon 'til 10 o'clock. That's when I remember waking up and I couldn't move. I was like, Fuck it, I'll just lay here. I woke up the next day at noon. I literally slept all the way from 3, 4 in the afternoon 'til noon the next day.

So I get up and I'm like, Okay well, I'm straight…I'm gonna take more. I took half the first day, then I took another half the second day. And the last thing I remember is trying to use the bathroom. I remember standing up to take a piss and I just fell over backward. Smack my back on the trash can, break the trashcan. And I get up again, and this time I fall over the other way, to the side. I remember that the bathroom floor was cold. And I remember trying to crawl over to a rug. I got to the rug, and that's the last thing that I remember. There are some things I have to keep to myself when telling this part of the story for personal reasons.

I woke up in the hospital. The doctor told me those mysterious new pills were methadone, which is used to wean heroin addicts off dope. Had I known it was methadone, I probably wouldn't have taken it. But as bad as I was back then, I can't even say 100 percent for sure.

I wasn't only depressed about Proof, I was depressed about my music in general. All I was taking was downers, strictly sedatives. My mood made my music depressing. And in turn, the depressing music made my mood depressed. My brain was thinking slow. My flow, my cadence, everything was just slow. Every record that I made was, Woe is me, and my life is so fucked and everything is wrong...

I overdosed, and I was in the hospital for a week detoxing. My doctor told me the amount of methadone I'd taken was equivalent to shooting up four bags of heroin. Even when they told me I almost died, it didn't click. I was pretty much in a coma for two days. All I remember was just peacefully sleeping and waking up in the hospital like, what the fuck is going on? There's tubes in me, there's all kinds of shit in me.

When you're told you almost died, in an addict's brain, this particular addict was thinking, Well, I didn't die, so I'm okay. WHEW! I got lucky. Thank you, God. God, please just please get me through this and I'll never use again.

*Eminem, "Can I Kick It?" *Vibe* interview, 2009

Eminem learned lessons the hard way. The thing that is in his heart and makes him tick is rap music. Eminem was supposed to come up with a *Relapse 2* album, but he changed his mind. His personal circumstances and artistic intent were different, so *Relapse 2* made less sense. After a few stays in rehab and some professional help, Marshall Mathers managed to stay clean for two years, which gave him some wings to spread in a new artistic direction. He gathered some new collaborators, worked on his new concept and *Recovery* was born:

I had originally planned for "Relapse 2" to come out last year. But as I kept recording and working with new producers, the idea of a sequel to "Relapse" started to make less and less sense to me, and I wanted to make a completely new album. The

> *music on "Recovery" came out very different from "Relapse",*
> *and I think it deserves its own title.*

Eminem's latest album to date, *Recovery*, was released in 2010. After experimenting with different styles and diverse English accents in *Relapse*, Eminem wanted to start something brand new. In *Recovery*, the artist is very lucid about his own mistakes. More introspective, Marshall Mathers decided to give his public a glimpse of the real him. No more evil Slim Shady disguise, no other character to spit his rage on *Recovery*. It is the real Marshall Mathers opening his heart to the public.

The very positive point of the whole album is certainly the return of the talented lyricist. As a matter of fact, many listeners felt let down by the artist since the release of Encore. They felt that album did not really meet the standards expected from a good hip hop album.

It is quite surprising that Eminem himself feels that his fans have been let down by the *Relapse* album, as he states it in his "Not Afraid" song:

> *And to the fans, I'll never let you down again, I'm back/I*
> *promise to never go back on that promise. In fact, let's be honest,*
> *that last Relapse CD was eh/Perhaps I ran them accents into*
> *the ground/Relax, I ain't going back to that now.*

Lyrically speaking, "Not Afraid" is interesting, because it stands for new artistic freedom and creativity. Eminem is ready to confront the music industry's dictatorships and to break free.

Before performing "Not Afraid" in Detroit City, Eminem paid some tribute to his fans:

> *Everybody in here who is an Eminem fan, man, I just want*
> *to take a minute out to say thank you. For the support that*
> *you all have shown me and for not giving up on me on some*
> *real shit, thank you, man. Especially you Detroit, I love you.*
> *This song is for you.*

Maybe Eminem was a little bit too harsh on himself. It is true that *Relapse* was quite surprising in its concept: Eminem took the risk for his album to be overlooked in its depth, even by die-hard fans.

The "On Fire" track unveils the artist's lyrical excellence: good beats, nice chorus, nice instrumentals, nice flow, and astute punch lines. In short, it reveals Eminem at his top level. The dark themes of rape and domestic violence are mentioned in "Love The Way You Lie," an artistic collaboration with Rihanna. One could be tempted to think that the song and video tend to glamorize domestic violence. A close, attentive look will teach the viewer that the song is all about preventing people, especially young ladies; against domestic violence. It clearly shows that violent men—despite all their vain promises—won't change.

From a critical point of view, there is a little bit too much of self-laceration in *Recovery*. Eminem's mood is morose and self-depreciating. Musically speaking, there are maybe too many rock 'n roll and metal influences in the latter album. Also, it is quite surprising to hear that a heavyweight in hip hop like Marshall Mathers admits envying Lil Wayne and Kanye West.

Rihanna and Eminem

From *Infinite* to *Recovery*, Marshall Mathers offers his audience a long path made of personal experiences and reflections. Wordsmith Eminem always was and will stay. Of course, Eminem has matured a lot, on a personal and artistic level. He has shown his public his great ability to experiment various and original instrumental and vocal combinations. He confronted his personal issues by a better self-understanding.

Of course, a lot of issues may remain unsolved for the artist, as he stated it in a 2010 *Rolling Stone* magazine interview:

> *I have trust issues. With women, friends, whatever. You always wonder what their real motives are. I've got a small circle of friends, and it's a lot of the same friends I've known forever. Right now, that works for me. I came out of some difficult things these past couple of years. I kind of feel like I'm just now finding my footing. So I want to make sure that's secure before I go out and do anything else. I need to keep working on myself for a while.*

Eminem's awareness of his issues is the first step towards his full personal recovery. Musically speaking, the artist is reborn from his ashes and ready to produce some more lyrical jewels, as he proved it with the release of his last album, *Recovery.*

Chapter 4

White Kid In A Black Music World

From Kansas City To Detroit

Marshall Mathers III was born in Saint Joseph, Missouri, near Kansas City, on October the 17th, in 1972. His mother, Debbie Mathers—Briggs married Marshall Mathers Jr. at the tender age of 15. She gave birth to Marshall when she was only 17. She almost died delivering a sick and fragile baby after 73 hours of labor.

Debbie and her husband also shared a common passion for music. They both were in a band called "Daddy Warbucks".

After Marshall was born, his parents moved to North Dakota, where his father was supposed to start a job as a hotel manager in his own father's (Eminem's paternal grandfather) company.

But things turned out sour very soon and in 1973, Debbie took her son back to Saint Joseph, Missouri, to live with his great aunt Edna Swartz (who passed away in 2006). Aunt Edna and Uncle Edmund Charles, as Eminem recalls in his *Evil Deeds* song in his "Encore" album, played a determinant role in Marshall's early education. Aunt Edna recalled these early childhood times* in a Kansas City TV interview. She had a lot of affection for Eminem and kept in contact with him till in her last days.

KC-TV5 News Kansas City, November 11. 2002

"I called him little Bruce. That just killed him. I still call him little Bruce".

She remembered how Marshall acted as a little boy:

And he had a little radio. We'd say: "Don't listen to that, Bruce. That's no good. He listened to it anyway.

Two years later Debbie would file for divorce, and the agreement left no visitation rights for Marshall's father. Marshall never saw his father again.

Due to the fact that he moved a lot back and forth between K.C. and Detroit; it was really difficult for little Marshall to make friends. Described as a *"shy and well behaved kid"*, young Marshall switched schools more than 20 times, which made it even more difficult to build true relationships.

When you're constantly on the move, stability seems to be a foreign word. You have to adapt to different types of environment very rapidly, which can cause some real discomfort for a real young kid.

Eminem tried to seek some comfort in a virtual world made of superheroes like Spiderman that he actually spent hours drawing. When he felt that his inside and outside worlds were endangered, Marshall Mathers could let his thoughts go like clouds in the wind and shelter in his fictional world.

He also liked to disguise and to play the superhero, which was a way to reassure him, as he became the target of some black kids teasing him at primary school.

A fat kid named D'Angelo Bailey

"There was a while when I was feeling like 'Damn, if I was just born black, I would not have to go through all this'"

Eminem

Marshall's outer world was insecure and made of daily trouble.

He was a small kid. Moreover, he was white. No need to explain that he was an easy target in a predominantly black area.

In 1981, when Marshall reached the age of 9, he was beaten up by a group of kids. The leader of these bullies, D' Angelo Bailey, two years older and a much bigger guy than him used to terrorize the small and shy Marshall at Roseville Elementary School. Talking about his victim, D'Angelo says: "He was small, plus he had a big mouth".

Legal sources *(Debbie Mathers sued her son's school) reveal four recorded incidents of Marshall getting beaten up:

- *On October 15th, 1981, he got beaten up, was bruised, and got the wind knocked out of him. The consequences were nausea and abnormal sleepiness. He also had injuries on his lips and tongue.*

- *Later November 14th, Marshall took another beating. He suffered from insomnia, vomiting, nightmares and antisocial behavior.*

- *Next episode would happen on December 21st: Marshall had injuries on his face, back and legs after another beating.*

- *But the worst was to come in 1982, on January 13th: Marshall was intentionally hit with a snowball containing a heavy object, was wounded severely while lying on the ground and went into a coma. He also suffered from intermittent loss of vision in his right eye combined with a loss of hearing at the time he woke up from coma.*

The Smoking Gun, Archives

When Marshall was transferred to the hospital, the doctors thought he was going to die. Surprisingly, he woke up 10 days later. His first words were: *"now I can spell elephant"*.

Because of her son's head injury and of the post beating symptoms he presented, Debbie Mathers tried to sue Roseville Elementary in 1982. Unfortunately, the lawsuit was dismissed in 1983.

Slim Shady, Marshall's evil alter ego, would take his revenge in the "Brain Damage" song in which the emcee narrates the tragic episode, adding some sarcastic verses that allow him to take advantage of his enemy D'Angelo Bailey:

> *I was harassed by that fat kid named D'Angelo Bailey/*
> *An eighth grader who acted obnoxious, 'cause his father boxes*
> *So every day he'd shove me into the lockers, and put me into*
> *a position to beat me into submission He banged my head*
> *against the urinal until he broke my nose*
> *Soaked my clothes in blood, grabbed me and choked my throat*

Probably full of resentment against his former victim's success and greedy about some possible financial gain, school bully D'Angelo tried to take Eminem to Court in 2001, claiming that the "Brain Damage" lyrics' purpose were only to increase the emcee's popularity.

In 2003, a judge named Deborah Servitto sarcastically dismissed D'Angelo's claim against Eminem. She made a good name for herself through this original and creative dismissal.

The originality of the judgment lies in its rhyming sentence:

> *Mr. Bailey complains that his rep is trash*
> *So he's seeking compensation in form of cash*
> *Bailey thinks he's entitled to some monetary gain*
> *Because Eminem used his name in vain*
> *Eminem says Bailey used to throw him around*
> *Beat him up in the john*
> *Eminem contends that his rap is protected*
> *By the right guaranteed by the first Amendment*
> *Eminem maintains that the story is true*
> *And that Bailey beat him black and blue*
> *In the alternative he states that the story is phony*
> *And a reasonable person would think it's baloney*

The Court must always balance the rights
Of a defendant and one placed in false light
If the plaintiff presents no question of fact
To dismiss is the only acceptable fact
If the language used is anything but pleasin'
It must be highly objectionable to a person of reason
Even if objectionable and causing offense
Self-help is the first line of defense
Yet Bailey actually spoke to the press
What do you think he didn't address?
Those false light charges that so disturbed
Prompted from Bailey not a single word
So highly objectionable it could not be
Bailey was happy to hear his name on a CD
Bailey also admitted he was a bully youth
Which makes what Marshall said substantial truth
This doctrine is a defense well known
And renders Bailey's case substantially blown.
The lyrics are stories no one would take as a fact
They're an exaggeration of a childish act
Any reasonable person could clearly see
That the lyrics could only be hyperbole
Is therefore this Court's ultimate position
That Eminem is entitled to summary disposition.

(Judge Deborah Servitto,
in D'Angelo Bailey vs. Marshall Mathers III case)

The Smoking Gun, archives

Debbie Mathers' testimony confirmed how serious her son's condition happened to be after the Roseville Elementary events back in 1982. It also makes you wonder why there was so much carelessness from school staff.

He was found in the bathroom, in blood, on the floor. Twenty
one doctors in four days gave up on Marshall.

The Smoking Gun, archives

The same D' Angelo guy attacked Marshall twice, as Debbie would confirm:

> *The first time was around Thanksgiving and the second time was around Christmas. Marshall had a slight concussion the first time. The second time he wasn't too lucky. Marshall fell in and out of consciousness.*

The doctors warned Debbie about the possibility of Marshall being a permanent patient in a psychiatric unit if he didn't recover his health. What mother wouldn't have felt desperate in such a crucial moment of her son's life?

> *It was the hardest thing for me to ever do. They gave me a choice-if Marshall's hearing didn't come back, his eyesight faded in and out—that I'd have to instutionalize him...*

A mother's heart always knows better. Debbie refused to give up on her son and courageously refused the doctor's advice, taking care of Marshall at home:

> *I refused to do so. He was on seizure and medications; he would black out and not even realize what he was doing at times. It took a year for him to bounce back.*

It is well known that brain and head injuries have a long lasting effect on people and it certainly affected Eminem's daily life for a while.

But his beating history didn't stop there. Marshall was to be confronted again with racism at the age of 16:

> *I was walking home from my boy's house, through the Bel-Air Shopping C, all these black dudes rode by in a car, flippin' me off. I flipped them off back, they drove away, and I didn't think nothing' of it. Evidently they parked the car. One dude came up, hit me in the face and knocked me down. Then he pulled out a gun. I ran right out my shoes, dog. I thought that's what they wanted. But they didn't.*

When Marshall returned the next day, his shoes were still stuck in the mud.

That's how I knew it was racial.

Eminem was lucky enough to find some white guy that day, who "had the guts" to pull his gun on the black men. He drove Marshall home.

About the incident, Debbie states:

He came just wearing his socks and underwear; they had taken his jogging suit off him, taken his boom box. They would have taken him out, too.

Ronnie was very influential to Marshall: they were like two brothers

Marshall's closest friend and biggest influence concerning rap happened to be Ronnie Dean Polkingharn. Ronnie Polkingharn was Betty Kresin (Eminem's grandmother's last son).

Ronnie Dean Polkingharn was Eminem's uncle, but both kids were nearly the same age and spent a lot of time playing together, mostly in Saint Joseph, Missouri.

Ronnie had a real passion for rap music and carried the strong dream to become a rapper. Ronnie also happened to love break dancing and would soon fully introduce Marshall to it.

Discovering "Reckless" by Ice T, both kids shared their passion for the music:

When I was 9 years old, my uncle put me on the Breaking soundtrack. The first rap song I ever heard was Ice T, Reckless. From LL to the Fat Boys, and all that shit, I was fascinated. When LL first came out with "I'm Bad", I wanted to be LL.

Eminem

Marshall, whose first ambition was to become a cartoonist; changed his mind at the age of 14; his devouring passion for rap music was taking over. During the time he spent in Saint Joseph, Ronnie and Marshall made rap tapes together.

Debbie's decision to return to Detroit City separated both friends.

Ronnie's dream to become a rapper never came true. Five years later, it was rumored that Ronnie committed suicide over a girlfriend. On December 13, 1991, Ronnie shot himself fatally at 19 years old, pointing a gun at his head, which left Marshall devastated. Totally depressed, he wasn't able to attend his uncle's funeral.

In fact, Eminem tried to end his days by swallowing pills that day, but fortunately survived his suicide attempt. During those months, he was giving up on his dreams, spending most of his time alone, and swallowing his pain.

The "Ronnie" tattoo is an eternal reminder of his dear uncle.

Ronnie's accidental death remains a mystery. According to Betty Kresin, her son was afraid of guns and would not have been capable of suicide. Her son's death spoiled her relationship with her grandson Marshall. Betty was upset that Marshall didn't attend the funeral.

Betty used to have a huge affection for Marshall. She totally turned against her grandson at this time. She accused him of changing for the worse. She turned down his request to put Ronnie's photo and a sample of his voice on his album. To the *Detroit News*, she angrily declared that she didn't want Marshall to destroy her dead son with this "garbage". This is probably how she perceived his music by then.

In response to her grimy declarations, Eminem told the same newspaper that he loved Ronnie (an undeniable fact) and that his only intent was to pay tribute to his uncle:

> *I loved Ronnie. I've got a Ronnie tattoo on my arm. I wanted to pay tribute to him. Nothing bad, I sell records regardless....*

Betty didn't seem to look at things the same way. She later changed her mind. In 2002 (according to Em72.com, 2002), Betty stood by her grandson. Expressing her pride, she understood that her grandson wanted to honor his best friend and uncle. She seemed to deeply regret the incident and affirmed that the only feud between her and Marshall was the use of Ronnie's voice.

Betty Kresin intended to write a tell-all book entitled the *Tie That Binds* in which she wanted to describe her family's story. Her book contains numerous references to Debbie's numerous boyfriends. She seems to remember one of them in particular, because of his destructive behavior:

> *Debbie had a lot of men in and out of her life. He went home and destroyed their duplex—even cutting up their king-sized waterbed. She called me crying asking me to help clean up the flood. All I could think about is 'Is my grandson ok?*

The book hasn't been released yet. Its aim is to give a clearer outlook on Eminem's family and the circumstances in which he grew up. Betty will also explain how she grew up as an unwanted kid with an alcoholic grandmother.

Marshall's roots

It is a well-known fact that Marshall Mathers has Scottish roots on his maternal grandmother's side and Scandinavian roots on his mother's paternal side. Eminem's father, Marshall Mathers II, comes from South Wales. Eminem's great-great-great grandmother, Ailsa Macalister (on Betty Kresin's side) was Scottish. Betty's great grandmother, Ailsa Mcalister was born in Edinburgh, in 1847. She immigrated to America and first went to New York, then moved to Kentucky two years later.

Welcome to Marshall's dysfunctional family

Unlike many other people that are currently involved in show business, Marshall Mathers didn't grow up with a golden spoon in his mouth. His upbringing was unstable, harsh and spoiled by a familial history of early marriages and numerous divorces, alcoholism, drug addiction, violence and abuse. These circumstances were transmitted from generation to generation and little Marshall inherited a chaotic internal world as a consequence.

His father's absence also impacted his daily life, with loads of deep bottled resentment after his letters to his dad came back to him, unanswered.

Eminem's grandmother: Betty Kresin

Betty used to live in Saint Joseph, Missouri. She married Bob Nelson when she was 14. She gave birth to her first child, her daughter Debbie in 1955. Then she decided to move back to Warren.

Despite the whirlwind of her constantly conflicted relationship to Bob, she had two more sons with him: Todd and Steven. The couple divorced in the 60's. Betty accused her former husband of verbal violence.

Betty soon met another man, Ron Gilpin, and had two more children with him. But Ron Gilpin was an alcoholic, which gave her second marriage very few chances of survival. Abandoned by her second husband, left with 5 children on her own, Betty struggled financially. She had to work two jobs in order to provide for her family.

In her teenage years, daughter Debbie attended St Joseph Central High School. Debbie was an attractive girl and soon her classmate Marshall Mathers II paid her some attention. Both became lovers. They later decided to get married. Debbie was only 15 when she married her 7 years older boyfriend, who was 22.

After two years of marriage, Debbie gave birth to Marshall III, in 1972. During the same period, Betty remarried for the third time. Ronnie was born shortly before Debbie had Marshall. Ronnie Dean Polkingharn was Betty's sixth child. Years later, in 1986, Debbie would give birth to her second child: Nathan.

Eminem's mom: Debbie Mathers

Although the real Debbie Mathers is somewhat unknown to the mainstream public, she is a pretty much-hated woman in Detroit and in the world.

Because her famous son put her on his records, dealing with their arguments publicly, Debbie Mathers has had really bad press, especially with Eminem's fans. From the Slim Shady LP to Relapse, Debbie's name is mentioned.

Debbie Mathers seems to have a quite complex personality. But to understand her behavior towards her son, the reader must understand that she is just a pure reflection of her environment. Coming from an unstable family background, nearly raped by her stepfather at the age of 12, and a history of addiction to painkillers.

This addiction probably made Marshall's childhood a living hell. But the element that hurt the mother-son relationship is the 10 million dollar lawsuit Debbie launched against her son when he had just reached fame. According to Debbie, the whole lawsuit is based on a huge misunderstanding. We may ask how a mom who pretends to love her son to that extent could be capable of suing him for money…

However, the public often misunderstands Eminem's relationship to his mother, despite its ups and downs. No matter how many times the artist would disrespect her on a record, at the end of the day; she remains his one and only mother.

"My fucking bitch mom is suing for 10 million" (Marshall Mathers song)

As Marshall's angry voice resonates on a guitar background, his sarcastic spirit unveils his mom's addiction history while many listeners, headphones on their ears, are smiling, catching the rapper's sense of humor with delight:

> *My fucking bitch mom suing for 10 million: she must want a dollar for every pill I been stealing*

Shit, where the fuck do you think I picked up the habit
All I had to do was to go to her room and lift a mattress

The original verse out of "My Name Is", that ignited the feud between Debbie and her son, is the following:

I just found out that my mom does more dope than I do.

Eminem states that his words are the reflection of the very truth:

As bizarre as my shit might be, it is still the reflection of the truth. When I say my mom does more drugs than me, people think I am just cracking jokes, but that shit is real. It's part of my childhood. 100% fucking true.

More elements also added fuel to the fire. In a June 1999 interview, published in *The Source Magazine,* entitled *"Fear of a White Rapper",* Eminem gave quantity of details about the circumstances that surrounded his childhood: the lack of financial means, growing up on welfare, bouncing from one place to another, the shame of having less than his friends, a fact that he was trying to constantly hide.

In America, there is a common misconception about white people being comfortable and all wealthy. Eminem breaks the stereotype with his own, realistic musical portrait.

Eminem's force as an artist is his capacity of presenting himself the way he is. He is one of the rare artists who doesn't provide a glamorous description of himself. He doesn't shy away from the dirty details, or even from calling himself *"white trash".* His honesty paid off and allowed him to win a public that is thirsty about authenticity.

Yeah, it's ha-ha funny, the stuff about my mom or father, but I don't know my fucking father. He abandoned us when I was 6 months old. My mom was about 16, 17 when she had me. It's all truth as warped as it sounds. People don't believe that white people are poor; they think white people just got it made. I was the poorest motherfucker on the block. I was the only white person on my block and the brokest. That's how I grew up on welfare. I'd hide the fucking welfare cheese under lettuce when my friends came over. Some were on welfare and some weren't, but I wanted to feel at least as good as everybody. I didn't wanna feel inferior. I would try to make our house look immaculate and shit. You know, you get made fun of it if you're on free lunch or your family is poor: like my mother would send me to the grocery store. I would steal the cigarettes and keep the 2 dollars she gave me so I could buy my lunch at school. I didn't want to be standing in line to sign free lunch voucher and you're in front of girls and shit. I'd be like 'Here you go. I'm paying for my own lunch. I do feel like I am coming from the standpoint where people don't realize there are a lot of poor white people. I kid you not; my family is fucking Jerry Springer, the epitome of white trash. Rap music kept my mind off the bullshit I had to go through. I kept my head up.

Eminem in *The Source Magazine,* 1999

In another *Rolling Stone* interview, Eminem underlined his hard childhood, his difficulty of getting involved in relationships because of his constant moves from Kansas City to Detroit and vice versa. Until they eventually got settled, when he was 12, stability sounded like utopia.

When his mom met somebody, they'd stay in Detroit. Marshall describes his mom's home as messed up. She kicked the habit and kicked her son out of the house, throwing dishes at him. He had just started working and part of his salary was meant to pay his mom's bills.

The numerous details Eminem gives us about his childhood show how much he suffered from the situation. Apparently, his mom didn't make any effort to get a proper job.

Another feud that opposed Eminem to his mom was the fact that he stopped paying the rent for her mobile home.

In September 2000, Marshall had a three-hour meeting with his lawyer that would be used in the trial for the 10 Million dollar defamation lawsuit.

In order to clarify some details about his mom's drug use—he had to specify that these drugs were prescription drugs (Valium, Vicatin)—which doesn't really change anything. Prescription drugs can get you hooked as fast as other drug pills.

Later on, Debbie made tremendous efforts to settle the 10 Million dollar lawsuit for 2 Million dollars, which her son declined immediately.

As a personal defense against the 10 million dollar lawsuit, Debbie stated:

> *I never intended to sue my son. The lawsuit was my attempt to hold on to my home. I'd given Marshall my trailer to rent when I moved back to Missouri. But Kim fell behind with the payments. I figured I had to sell it to pay the debt, but she wouldn't let me. She threatened me with a lawyer, so I consulted one myself. Then the whole thing just escalated. The first thing I knew, I swear, was when Marshall rang me and said, 'Mom, why are you suing me for $10 million?' I nearly fell over. It was ludicrous. Then word got out and the world saw me as an evil bitch from hell. What mother sues her son? I was cursed in public, spat at in shopping malls.*

Paul Rosenberg, Eminem's manager, backed the artist's statements confirming that they are a 100% true.

In 2002, Eminem shared an argument he had with his mom (back in the days when his uncle Ronnie died) in his song, "Cleaning Out My Closet" from *The Eminem Show*.

The artist reveals that Debbie said some hurtful words aimed at her son during this argument that opposed mother and son. When Ronnie died, she said she wished it was Marshall:

> *Bitch do your song - keep tellin yourself that you was a mom!*

But how dare you try to take what you didn't help me to get
You selfish bitch; I hope you fuckin burn in hell for this shit
Remember when Ronnie died and you said you wished it was me?
Well guess what, I AM dead—dead to you as can be!

Eminem, "Cleaning Out My Closet"

Debbie might have been hurt by Marshall's words. Her harmful words towards her son, though, are like a sharp sword "*shanking*" somebody's heart.

About this terrible argument opposing her to her son, Debbie Mathers told Camille Dodero in 2008:

> *It's something I will regret till my dying day.*

The Village Voice Blog, December 2008

Drug problems put aside, Debbie's Munchhausen syndrome (an illness in which the mother makes her own kid believe that he is sick and puts him on medication in order to raise people's attention) influenced her behavior towards her son.

There are also references about Debbie's Munchhausen syndrome in Eminem's "Cleaning Out My Closet" song:

> *Now I would never diss my own momma just to get recognition*
> *Take a second to listen for who you think this record is dissin*
> *But put yourself in my position; just try to envision*
> *Witnessin your momma poppin prescription pills in the kitchen*
> *Bitchin that someone's always goin throuh her purse and shit's missin*
> *Goin through public housin systems, victim of Munchausen's Syndrome*
> *My whole life I was made to believe I was sick when I wasn't*
> *'Til I grew up, now I blew up, it makes you sick to ya stomach*
> *Doesn't it? Wasn't it the reason you made that CD for me Ma?*

Eminem, "Cleaning Out My Closet"

The official of Saint Clair Shores* thought that she had Munch-hausen's syndrome while observing her attitude towards her second boy Nathan. In 1996, Nathan was removed from her custody. Among other details, it was discovered that her personality was almost paranoid. Apparently, Debbie had forbidden her son to play with other kids. She regained the custody of her son one year later, though.

ABC News, September 2000

Another website called *Salon Dot Com* confirms that Nathan Mathers was removed from his mother's custody for a year approximately, in 1996:

> *But the most damning accusation came from St. Clair Shores school officials, who in juvenile court proceedings in 1996 accused her of abusing her younger son, Nathan, now 14. Nathan was removed from her custody. Alleging that she "exhibits a very suspicious, almost paranoid personality," a social worker suggested that Mathers-Briggs had Munchausen syndrome by proxy, an affliction in which a parent injures a child to gain attention and sympathy for herself.*
>
> *School officials also said she accused neighbors of beating Nathan, blowing up her mailbox and killing her dog in a satanic ritual. They added that she told them video cameras were monitoring her from trees outside her house and that enemies had sent her a tarantula in the mail.*
>
> *Mathers-Briggs pleaded no contest to reduced charges that she was emotionally unstable and had failed her son by keeping him out of school and isolating him from other children; with that, she regained custody. By then, Nathan had been in foster homes for more than a year.*
>
> *Attorney Betsy Mellos, who represented Mathers-Briggs through much of the court battle, says the school brought the charges because the mother had threatened to sue them. "She was a pretty good mother," contends Mellos, who now prosecutes*

child abuse and neglect cases for Macomb County, Mich. "If anything, she was overprotective".

Salon Com, "Eminem's Dirty Secrets",
July 2000, M.L Elrick

It is quite obvious that the mother-son relationship deteriorated to the worst since Eminem's success:

> *Ever since my success, shit hasn't been all good with me and her. She wants to act like it is, and talk all that shit about I love my son, and this is just a lesson he's gotta learn. I love my son, but I am suing him for $10 Million. In other words, I'm trying to take everything he's worked away from him, but I love my son. C'mom, man gimme a fucking break.*

Debbie Mathers' side of the story

Many fans of her son made her life a living hell, because they didn't understand that Eminem's public arguments with his mother were not addressed to them personally. Sometimes, it is real good to make a straight separation between entertainment and reality. Spitting at Debbie Mathers at the supermarket is kind of surrealistic. Why would people hate a woman they don't even know? Why would they try to interfere between Marshall and his mom? Maybe is time to understand that Eminem's public issues with his family members are none of our business.

> *When my son Marshall—that's his name, not Eminem—first got into rap as a teenager he would wake me at 5:00am to ask me words that rhymed with what. I bought him a dictionary and it all went downhill from there.*

> *Because of what Marshall has written, to his fans I am the most hated person on this planet. I've been spat on by kids in the supermarket. Yet I do know him, probably better than anyone, and I want to try and explain to his fans—and all the parents who I know are horrified by the lyrics of to his songs—what makes my son tick.*

"Dear Marshall"

In a probably desperate reconciliation attempt towards her son, Debbie Mathers released a three song CD with the artists X-ID. Whether you consider this song as a fabricated sob story to win the public's attention or as a desperate plea from a mother towards her son, the lyrics to the song will allow the listener to make up his own mind. The song is written in a spoken mode, which invites the listener to catch up with each of Debbie's words and give them a more attentive listen. Of course, Debbie's intentions to win all mothers hearts is quite obvious, if you consider the tone in which she addresses the public:

Dear Marshall,

I just want to start by saying I still love you. Even when I was pregnant with you, it was very hard for me.

The 72 hours of torture was worth every minute of it. When I looked into these big blue eyes, this was the first time I ever felt true love in my whole life.

We have a problem, Marshall.

The past two years something really went wrong. I was so excited about your success, yet let down by your betrayal. Playing the role of both dad and mom must've taken more of a toll on you that I ever imagined.

Marshall, I did the best I could. I went without so you could have. It was wrong of me and I see it now, as giving you everything and never questioning anything you did, as you were perfect in my eyes. My unconditional love created a spoiled man and an angry one.

Now, before God and everyone, I must apologize 'cause at the time I felt it was the right thing to do.

I'm tortured daily, Marshall, by people asking me why you're such an angry young man. Being the only role model in your life, of course, they're going to blame me." Their demeaning me needs to stop and I speak for lots of mothers. The words really hurt and they cut like a knife with no way to mend a bleeding heart. If not for my friends who have been there for me, and yes, Marshall, they really truly care.

I pray someday you're not gonna be alone and you'll have friends like me. They won't be there just for your fame. And no more vicious attacks on me and vicious acts of hate; 'Cause it really hurts. Will the real Marshall Mathers please stand up and take responsibility for his actions?

And I am going to close this, Marsh, by saying it's not too late to change.

As always, sincerely, your only mother.

Debbie Mathers might describe her son as angry. However, his anger didn't just surface ex nihilo. Despite his rough childhood and the way he was treated as a kid, Eminem seemed to have made efforts towards certain normality in his relationship to his mother.

All of a sudden his mother is suing him for $10 Million when he becomes famous over one line in a song. In addition to all this, she is telling her son that she'd prefer him to die instead of Ronnie during an argument, as stated in Eminem's "Cleaning Out My Closet" song.

As a matter of fact Debbie sued her son for a total amount of $12 Million, but then settled for $25,000. But then again, in June 2001, Debbie changed her mind, determined to sue her son again.

Macomb Circuit Court judge Switalski ruled it as impossible:

If someone feels subsequent to it, it doesn't change that it's a settlement, established in by writing agents of the two parties.

One could justifiably question Debbie's real motivation behind the lawsuits.

Anybody with a normal brain would react badly to Debbie's behavior. When you worked like a slave and eventually see your dream come true, the person that is the closest to your heart comes and is trying to steal what you worked for, how could you *not feel angry?*

A part of Debbie probably still loves her son and she is desperately trying to win his heart by any means, even if that meant stalking her son at Christmas while staying in a Detroit motel.

In order to plead her cause in front of a whole audience and spectators, Debbie became the guest on the *Sally Raphael Show* in March 2001. Accompanied by her son Nathan, she spoke out in a very contradictory way. Her son Marshall who was *"constantly demeaning his mother in his songs"* suddenly became *"an OK young man who worked very hard and who'd give anybody the shirt off his back"*.

Eminem's dropped a sarcastic answer to his mother's appearance to the *Sally Raphael Show* in his *Without Me* video, disguised like Debbie *"going to the messy sally lesbial show"*, where *"sons go bad"*. The video features Marshall's little brother Nate.

The video was very hilarious. Maybe not for Debbie, though.

From Debbie's point of view, Marshall's dirty lyrics's aim is commercial:

> *He is making money out of negative issues because he could not make it as a rap star in any other way. When he first started to write dirty lyrics I asked him why. His answer was the more foul he was the more people loved him. He didn't make money out of nice things. If he wrote a song about how much he loved his mother and little brother, he'd be laughed at.*

Rap music, is, in its essence, rebellious and angry. It is the reflection of ghetto life. In that way, Debbie Mathers is certainly right. However, it would have been very risky for Marshall Mathers to lie about his past, particularly as a white artist in a black dominant musical genre.

A lot of people—including Debbie's former boyfriends—have witnessed the way she behaved towards her son Marshall—which doesn't favor her version of the facts.

In another interview given to Amy Reiter in 2001, Debbie Mathers points out that her son simply made up his rough childhood for his career's sake:

> *He said to me, "Mom, black people do not believe that there are poor white people out there, that we have to struggle too and work. They think that we're born with a silver spoon in our mouth. And I have to say something. I can't just say, 'Well, I was overprotected by my mom. And my mom tried to give me everything.' Because they already think that. They already think that white people have everything."*

"A Conversation with Eminem's Mom",
Amy Reiter, *Salon.Com*, February 2001

Ironically Debbie's own mom, Betty, who turned against Marshall once, doesn't back her daughter at all regarding the lawsuit:

> *I turned my back on my daughter. If you don't drop that lawsuit, I'm going to come to your house, run you over and go to prison myself. How can you do that to your own son? This kid has done nothing to nobody. He grew up very hard, my daughter moved a lot and she had a lot of boyfriends. Debbie is not the best mother.*

According to Betty, her daughter likes feuds and seems to be used to lawsuits:

> *Oh, I'll figure she'll sue me. She's always going to sue somebody.*

In "Cleaning Out My Closet," Eminem defines his childhood this way:

> *Kicking ass in the morning and taking names in the evening.*

With his lyrical brilliance, one would agree that Eminem doesn't really need to disrespect his own mother to get recognition and respect from his public.

In "Cleaning Out My Closet" again, the rapper addresses to his listeners:

> *Now I would never dis my own mama to get recognition/ take a second to listen if you think this record is dissing.*

Debbie's opinion about "Cleaning Out My Closet" (obviously) differs:

> *He's got a persona to live up to, an image. That's just artistic expression, he's very sad on the inside. He's hurting a lot. And I can see it. I can see through my son. I know him like the back of my hand.*

As much as it is true that image is everything in the music industry, why would an artist spend so much time washing his dirty laundry in public when he could easily disrespect any rival rapper with his high level of skills?

If Debbie doesn't take her son's rhymes literally, why on earth does she seem so much hurt by them?

Is Eminem a puppet into the music industry's hands? Debbie seems to believe it:

> *The minute you start becoming destructive and being different—you know, kill your mother, rape this one and kill that one—I mean, people love it. He's got everybody pulling him in different directions: managers, different people, telling him what to say. And money is power, you know.*

Debbie is pretty much aware of the way the music industry works. The label, the manager, the producer and many other collaborators are pushing the artist into the direction they want him to follow. The publicist will do anything possible to reflect a positive image of his protégé. This is absolutely true. However, Eminem as an artist doesn't seem to fake feelings or emotions. His life portrayal since he started rapping is a quite realistic image of what he has been trough.

It is interesting to note that Debbie could be convincing if only she recognized a few mistakes from the past. But it looks like she needs to live up to the image of the 'perfect parent'. Life in itself will prove to mankind that there is no perfect parenting at all. Every mom on earth does mistakes, but not every mom will admit it easily, particularly when her conscience tells her she is wrong.

Including her former boyfriends, a lot of people seem to have confirmed Debbie's temper tantrums and her quite obvious addiction to drugs.

In his *Relapse* album, Marshall Mathers wrote another song about his mom, but in a very different spirit. Drugs nearly killed the talented artist in December 2007. He eventually realized where his addiction history lies in his family. He understood the difficulties his mom was facing with her own addiction and showed some more compassion. Despite the ironic tone of My Mom, this song might be a first step towards a further reconciliation.

Eminem is unique in his way of sharing emotions with his listeners. Where he experienced pain in his past, he wants the listener to walk through his path of pain and to imagine him as a small child, longing for security and comfort and missing love from his mother's side.

At the same time, his music is a powerful outlet for his pain and frustrations, but he also seems to confide in the person who is listening to him, sharing emotions and pain, creating a special bond with the fan or listener.

In 2006, the press spilled a lot of ink about Debbie Mathers' apparent sickness. A lot of tabloids were reporting that "Eminem's dying mom" was seeking reconciliation with her son, uttering that she was in a terminal phase of breast cancer. In fact, Debbie had been misdiagnosed. A few years later, she was dealing with breast cancer for real, according to her own statements:

> *I'm still under doctor's care, which I probably will be for a while. Basically a lot of the stuff is hereditary, but that happens. Cancers and heart disease and all that, and all the genetic things. I worry about my boys, having high-blood pressure and things.*

Debbie Mathers, interview with Camille Dodero, 2008)

While Eminem was releasing a memoir entitled *The Way I Am* in October 2008, a tell-all book containing some exclusive, unreleased material in which he unveils more about his character, admitting openly his temper issues, for instance, Debbie Mathers also released a book the same year called *My Son Marshall, My Son Eminem..* In her book, Debbie Mathers gives details about her own life and how, according to her, her son Marshall built up a bunch of lies about his life in order to access fame.

Debbie's book is also enriched with some rare pictures, and unreleased Eminem lyrics and poems. Her clear intent is to set the record straight about Eminem's former lyrics. She wants to defend herself and prove that she has been a good mother to her son:

> *At first, I went along with it for Marshall's sake—if I made one mistake as a mother, it was giving in to my eldest son's every whim. He never knew his father and I did all I could to make up for it. I wasn't happy when he made up a whole new life for himself—what mother wants to be known as a pill-popping alcoholic who lives on welfare?*

Debbie brands her son a liar:

> *To tell the truth, I was heartbroken. The lies started coming thick and fast—and not just from Marshall. I think he's forgotten the good times we had, and this book is my way of setting the record straight.*

In a rare interview given to Camille Dodero on December 4, 2008 that was leaked on the *Village Post* Blog, Eminem's mom gave a few

more updates about the intentions behind her book release, her
health state, and her relationship with her son and granddaughter.

In July 2008, Debbie accidentally saw her eldest son at the
Cemetery in Saint Joseph, Missouri while visiting Ronnie's grave:

> *They called me at the cemetery because there were all these people
> who showed up there. They weren't sure who they were, and they
> were looking for my little brother Ronnie's grave. The cemetery
> had a lot of people tearing up gravesites and they wanted to make
> sure the visitors were authentic and things like that.*
>
> *Eminem's bodyguard got out of a van and gave me Marshall's
> phone number and said, "Mom, you should call me sometime.
> His bodyguard said your son's in the next vehicle, you need
> to say 'hey' to him." And I went to, but Tracy floored it and
> went around.*
>
> *I was kinda hurt. It would have been good. I didn't even see him
> sitting there. The windows were tinted; I could see through them
> a little bit, but I didn't even see him sitting in the back seat.
> So he must've been, like, kneeling down or in the floorboard.*

Debbie also insisted on the fact she is constantly sending checks
to Marshall and Hailie on specific occasions like birthdays, for
instance:

> *Well, for the holidays, and for his birthday and things, because
> he doesn't really buy himself that much, it doesn't matter how
> much the check is for. It's just the principle of letting him know
> I'm thinking of him and to go buy himself something nice and,
> actually, that he needs to stop buying for everybody else.*

Eminem's *The Way I Am* offers a lot of lucid insights about his
family's abuse history. Through Eminem's own effort for a better
self-understanding, it also makes the reader's task easier to picture
the environment that made Eminem become the person he is now.

My Son Marshall, My Son Eminem sold over 100 000 copies in
the UK. However, the publication of her book was stopped in the

United States. Neal Alpert, who helped Debbie with the book, decided to sue her, because he never received his 25% part of the sales benefits. Apparently, both parties settled their disagreements. In 2009, *Radar Online* reported Debbie Mathers' plans to marry her agent, Neal Alpert. Neal is said to be bisexual, but this doesn't come into play in her marriage and relationship with her partner:

> *When it comes to marriage it's not about the sex, it's about being with your best friend. He has always been a gentleman and respectful and never sold her out for a penny, even when he had the chance.*
>
> Debbie Mathers

In 2009, Debbie was reported to be dying of breast cancer, but we can assume that she might well have recovered, or at least she must be doing better: the *Oakland Press* revealed that she released a single on You Tube called "Nobody Likes A Bully" in collaboration with her partner Neal Alpert in January 2012.

Both partners are involved in an anti-bullying campaign. Neal Alpert commented on the video:

> *I've been watching the bullying issue unfold for a few years now, and I wanted to do something about it, I communicated with Debbie, who also expressed much interest, about collaborating on something to get the message out against it. I was the victim of bullying while attending school, and Debbie was the victim of domestic abuse growing up. We felt with Debbie being thrust into the spotlight regarding her famous son and the film '8 Mile,' we could use her celebrity for a good cause. Based on my own past experience with bullying and Debbie's past with abuse, we ultimately hope it makes a connection with students. Nobody should have to ever go through life feeling victimized.*
>
> *Oakland Press*, 2012

The video features Michigan rap artist, Sir K.

Eminem's *The Way I Am* offers a lot of lucid insights about his family's abuse history. Through Eminem's own effort for a better self-understanding, it also eases the reader's mind to picture the environment that made Eminem become the person he is now. Developing more insight about family abuse history, Eminem is working on breaking the cycle within his own family.

It is quite interesting to note that mother and son, while taking different directions, are both working on better self-awareness.

Debbie's boyfriends and husbands

A lot of men were present in Debbie's life, but it sometimes seems hard to say how much they impacted little Marshall's life and how many of them could be considered as a "father figure".

Don De Marc used to be Debbie's boyfriend in the late 70s and early 80s. He helped Debbie raising Marshall and states that the little boy used to test his limits.

He also talked about Debbie's drug abuse:

> *She complained of headaches, backaches and toothaches, she always seems to be in pain. She's always looking for pain pills.*

Donald De Marc* also remembers Marshall as a kid. According to him, the young boy started rapping at the age of 5:

> *He was a rhymer. He would sit there and driving down the street, he would always come up with something. We would hear songs on the radio and he would change words around.*
>
> *Salon.Com, Arts and Entertainment,* July 25,2000

Such precocity is quite impressing. It is quite obvious that Eminem was born with a musical gift and a magical ability to juggle words like a circus acrobat.

His mom Debbie would also confirm her son's musicality:

> *Marshall was very different. Marshall had always liked to bounce. He liked to bounce a lot. I mean sitting on a chair against the wall, on a couch, a car…a lot of people thought he was maybe retarded in school, because he bounced off his desk.*

Of course, Don De Marc also recalls rough moments in little Marshall's life, but he also remembers the happy moments with the little boy:

> *When I kissed him good night, we'd say 'goodnight, goodnight', don't let the bed bugs bite'. One would say all right. The other one would say all wrong.*

Fred Samra, Nate's father, whom Debbie sued for child support, confirms Debbie's addiction and things Marshall went through:

> *She's lying about the drug and stuff, I won't say any more. You would not believe the shit he's been through.*

In a *Detroit Free Press* article from November the 24, 1999, Berger Olsen Au Gres, who happened to be married to Debbie from 1988 to 1990, describes the way Debbie used to treat her son in his presence:

> *She was throwing him out of the house all the time. I remember Marshall telling her: 'I want to rap, and when I do I will do one all about you.'*

As a matter of fact, Debbie's conflicted relationship to her daughter in law, Kimberley Scott, didn't ease the situation. We also need to underline that Kim's presence in Debbie's home is prior to her dating Marshall. She used to live there as Marshall's foster sister, because she went from a violent, broken place and had no other place to go.

If Eminem's only goal was to make money, he could have stopped straight after the release of the Slim Shady LP.

The main reason Eminem started rapping is his passion for the music and his great ability to play with words. Anybody who is conscious of his gift knows he has to develop it the best he can. This kind of gift is like a little grain you'd plant in your garden, spill water on it daily until it becomes a magnificent tree bearing the most succulent fruit.

Both Eminem and his mom have been through a lot of trouble and difficult situations.

Absent from the scene since 2005 after the cancellation of his European Tour, and being so close to death because of his pill addiction; Marshall Mathers had enough time for some personal introspection. Now that he is sober, he has become conscious of the huge pill addiction problem he had and realized that his mom suffered from the same kind of problem.

Let's hope a new chapter will open, in which there might be a space for reconciliation between mom and son.

A lot of Eminem fans often think that Debbie is in the wrong when she talks about her son. Although she might be wrong on some precise points, she remains his mother. Your mom is one of the people in your life who usually knows you better than the rest of the world.

And regardless of the "disses" Eminem might have thrown at his mom's face on his records, to quote the man himself, 'at the end of the day, she remains my mom'.

That's why the fans and the average listener should avoid making fast judgments.

Behind the story: Debbie Mathers' sickness

> *"…victim of Munchausen's syndrome, my whole life I was made to believe I was sick when I wasn't'till I grew up"*
>
> Eminem, "Cleaning Out My Closet"

Here are the words that describe Eminem's mom's shady behavior towards her son. In "Cleaning Out My Closet", words are dropped like a menacing tornado. The artist takes his revenge from a hurtful past—at least lyrically.

The music is his best way to deal with his demons from the past. However, these ghosts from the past are very difficult to blow away, as they might reappear during bad times or while you're insecure in order to mess with your mind. That's why it is so difficult for Eminem to sometimes reach a peace of mind he's been longing for:

> *Yeah, it's a harsh record but I feel my mother has done some harsh things to me. You just try your whole life to get away from that person and make a life for yourself and not really deal with it anymore. And it's so hard to break away. And they keep coming back to haunt you, trying to weasel their way into your life somehow. That's my closure song, I guess. I'm washing my hands of it. I'm cleaning out my closet. I'm done.*

The wounds parents inflict on their kids are really hard to cure. It is probably because they are so close to us and will—whether we like it or not—influence our first perceptions of the world and our personality.

It can be so hard to forgive your own mother, because some wounds might continue to bleed.

What exactly is Munchausen's syndrome?

Munchausen's syndrome can be defined as a psychological illness. It was discovered in 1977. A person with that kind of illness gives fake symptoms of illness and insists that she is sick. This kind of sickness can also take the form of child abuse. This particular sickness is called Munchausen's syndrome by proxy.

The mother makes her own child believe that he's sick and convinces him to take some medication that will generate other symptoms such as vomiting. This kind of behavior from the mother towards her child can lead to the death of her child.

Munchausen's syndrome by proxy is a serious condition, which explains partly Debbie's behavior.

In a *Rolling Stone* interview from 1999, Eminem explains how his mom got him hooked on drugs:

In Court, I had to testify against her. Nate, who was 9 at the time, was too scared to testify against our mom. My mother made me believe he was a hyperactive kid and that he was suffering from Attention Deficit Disorder. My mother said I was a hyperactive kid and I wasn't. She put me on Ritalin.

Ritalin is a drug that is usually used as a prescription for hyperactive kids. The constant combination of Valium, Ritalin and Vicodin can lead to addiction, over sedation, respiratory depression. It can also lead a person to his final fate.

How insecure Marshall's world must have felt, with his own mother making an addict of him. There are no words to describe such abuse.

We might raise the question of Debbie's real guilt. How could she be considered guilty when she is really sick? The way she acted must have been at least partly unconscious.

However, the consequences of her behavior are still there. She messed with his body and mind. The scars of the past are sometimes hard to heal.

Marshall's father

When you see my Dad, tell him that I slit his throat in this dream I had.

Eminem, "My Name Is"

My father? I never knew him. Never seen a picture of him.

Eminem on his Dad

According to the common story, Marshall Bruce Mathers II went out of his son's life when he was only 6 months old.

Little Marshall had contact with his paternal grandmother Rae. As a five-year-old, he wrote a card destined for her. Grandma Rae also kept records of Marshall's evolution as a baby.

According to Betty Kresin, young Marshall used to draw some pictures and asked his family to give them to his dad.

Despite that, the young kid had no contact with his father who moved to California. Was it because this contact was denied to him? Or was it simply because his father wasn't keen on a relationship with his son?

Apparently, Marshall's family was aware of his dad's address. As a young teenager, he wished to get in touch and send some letters to his dad. Every single letter came back with the mention: "Return To Sender".

Strange and hurtful silence from a man who suddenly shows up when his "lost son" becomes overwhelmingly famous…His father-less past affected Eminem to a great extent.

Marshall Mathers II gave an interview in the *Daily Mirror*. Like Debbie, he wrote an open letter to his son that was published around 2002 in the English tabloid:

Hello son. You won't remember me, though I held you in my arms when I was a baby. You think I dumped you and your mother and never came looking for you. You're convinced I'm a drunk who never answered one of your letters. Well, I want you to read this and realize you've been fed lies all your life, Now you'll hear the truth for the first time.

The one ambition left in my life is to give you a hug and tell you I've always loved you. I'd get on a plane right now, this second, and go anywhere in the world you'd meet with me. Please get in touch."

Eminem's dad was first informed about Marshall's whereabouts by his son Michael. Then his daughter Sarah brought him a Rolling Stone magazine in which Eminem was featured. The magazine had included a photo of young Debbie holding her son. Michael, my other son, came to our house one day and asked me what his half-brother's name was. He's seen a clip of Eminem on MTV.

I told him it was Marshall and he said I might like to sit down because he had something to tell me. At first I just thought it was a coincidence. Then about two months later "Rolling Stone" magazine did a big article on him.

My daughter Sarah brought the article and it was a picture of Debbie holding Marshall as a baby. I thought 'Oh my God, so much for a coincidence.' I was just stunned. First of all I was really grateful he was alive; that was the main thing.

I had no idea what had gone on. Then, to have all that recognition on top, I was flabbergasted. It is still hard to believe...

With a non-hidden emotion, Marshall Mathers II talks about the notebook he discovered at his mother Rae's home:

It was Eminem's grandmother, my mother Rae, who had held onto this book.

We only found it after she went into a care home with Alzheimer's disease. I had to go to her house and find health insurance papers and other documents...Looking through all her stuff we found the book with old photographs and a Christmas card Marshall sent her when he was five.

Eminem's dad describes his son as a "happy, curious baby". The lately discovered baby book reveals many interesting details about the rapper's early childhood, including little Marshall's hand and foot ink prints when he was only a few weeks old.

Eminem's dad also possesses other treasures of emotions like his son's maternity bracelet, a lock of baby hair and a photo album of his early years.

Although he doesn't earn much as a steelworker, Eminem's dad insisted that he's not interested in his son's money.

I don't want to see a cent of Marshall's money. He has become famous and I've found out where he is. It doesn't mean I've found a meal ticket.

Amy Reiter, an online writer for "Salon People" (a website), adds sarcastically:

> *And while you're at it, if you could see fit to send him a plane ticket, arrange him a limo meet him at the airport, put him at the airport, to put him up at a four star hotel room, take him out for a fancy meal (or at least some donuts) and provide him a few backstage passes; I am sure he'd be grateful.*

Without putting a specific intent of sarcasm on our side, Eminem's dad's sincerity might be questionable, as he resurfaces all of a sudden when his son becomes famous. We haven't seen him prove his good intentions yet.

Why search your son so many years after his disappearance? Why is there a lack of response to his son's letters when he needed him most?

Marshall Mathers II pretends that he never wanted to leave his family. He puts the fault on Debbie who left an empty apartment, leaving her past behind.

While it seems quite obvious that Debbie must have manipulated her former husband, reemerging when his son becomes famous is highly suspicious. Using the tabloids as a public way of communications might indicate some hidden greed for money and a wish for attention from the media.

Marshall Mathers II also expressed his wish to see Hailie, his only grandchild to date in 2002. (In the meantime, his other son has had two daughters.)

Eminem's dad is determined not to give up on meeting his "lost son":

> *Until we meet, there will always be something missing in my life. As long I am still alive and kicking I'll be knocking on the door to see if I get any answers. I am certain that one day it will happen.*

One could barely tell if his feelings are genuine or not, but the man expressed his pain about the situation. However, it would be clever to question if he ever envisioned the huge inner pain he inflicted on his son by his absence and lack of communication during his childhood and teenage years.

In a *60 Minutes* TV interview that goes back to October 11, 2011 Eminem clearly stated that there are no chances for a reunion with his father*:

> *I never knew him, I never met him, I never knew him. I don't know if I want to see him. Some people ask me that and I don't think I do. I can't understand how he could leave. If my kids moved to the edge of the earth, I'd find them. No doubt in my mind. No money, no nothing. If I had nothing, I'd find my kids, so there is no excuse.*
>
> Eminem, Pacific Coast News, October 11, 2011

Other family members are trying to cash in on Eminem's fame

> *For every million I make, another relative sues*
> *Family fighting and fussin*
> *Over for who wants to invite me to supper*
> *All of a sudden I got 90 some cousins (Hey it's me)*
> *A half brother and sister who never seen me*
> *Or even bothered to call me*
> *Until they saw me on TV*
>
> "Marshall Mather's" song

The more famous, the wealthier Eminem becomes, the greedier relatives prey on the talented emcee. It must be really lonely at the top, because close family members who are supposed to support you suddenly turn against you and become your worst enemies.

She used to be that close to the Mathers family that she was babysitting Hailie at the time Eminem was acting in his "8 Mile" movie. A picture, taken around 2001-2002, proves that she knew Brittany Murphy personally.

Married, with 3 kids, she desperately tried to have a threesome with Eminem and Kim. Her kids used to call Eminem "Uncle Marshall".

Who is this mysterious woman? Her name is J.R Watkins, Kim's cousin, a barely educated woman with rude (and cheap) manners.

Another of her publicity stunts—after being kicked out of the Mathers' house—was to pretend she was being forced to have an abortion, because she was carrying Marshall's baby.

In 2002, when Eminem was celebrating his 30th birthday, he had to call Detroit Station in the "Mojo In The Morning Show" to clear the air about some dirty rumors regarding the rapper himself and his ex-wife Kim. The public also learned during that audio session that J.R Watkins intended to write a book about Eminem.

About JR Watkins, Eminem specified:

> *The people who end up writing books about me, end up in their trailer trash homes anyway.*

Him and Kim

> *Me and Kim, we been through our dramas and shit, but I'd be bald faced if I said I don't love her or I'm with her because of my daughter. I'm with her, 'cause I really wanna be with her. I love that girl, man. I really do.*

Eminem on Kim

Marshall Mathers and Kimberley Scott's relationship escapes any random rules. The closest definition of their love-hate relationship would be: *"I can't live with or without you."* Constantly on and off (the couple married and divorced twice), a mixture of burning passion and deep hatred, Eminem and Kim's relationship is really complex. It would be foolish for any observer to jump to conclusions.

Kimberley Ann Scott is probably Marshall's best (female) friend and enemy. Debbie adopted Kim as Marshall's foster sister when she was only 13. Marshall started dating Kim when he was around 15.

Marshall recalls the first time he met his sweetheart Kim:

She was visiting my friend's sister. My friend had a stereo, and whenever his mom used to leave for work, we'd get it out and hang out there. We would just put the stereo on blast and play all the new shit. I had a red Kangol on. I was jumping on the coffee table, singing along to an LL song. I was really into it. I kinda saw her come in the doorway out of the corner of my eye. I just kept going; showing off. She watched until I finished the song. And then my friend's sister introduced us.

The Source, May 2002

Eminem's mom is known for being a manipulative and controlling person. Her complex personality might have influenced Kim to a great extent. Some people from Eminem's former entourage, like Byron Williams (Eminem's former bodyguard) who had the chance to approach Kim would say that *she is his mom reincarnated.*

As a matter of fact, to the close observer, Kim knows perfectly where to *"push the buttons"* in order to obtain a specific reaction from Marshall.

This is how she managed to use the couple's daughter Hailie as a weapon that would tear them apart.

In 1995, Kim got pregnant and gave birth to their daughter Hailie Jade, on December 25, 1995.

Hailie's birth acted like a spring renewal into Marshall's life, particularly after Ronnie's death and the years of depression that followed.

It also gave Eminem a new sense of responsibility, as he wanted to break from his family's history. Unlike his own father, he wanted to care for his daughter and to be there for her.

His more stable place of work was a restaurant called *"Gilbert's Lodge"*, where he often worked on extra shifts. Eminem happened to be a quite unconventional and original worker. He often exasperated his boss, because he was always rapping the commands.

Eminem and Kim lived in a bad neighborhood where burglaries and gunshots were common:

The neighborhoods we lived in fucking sucked, I went through four TVs and VCRs in two years.

Once, a thief came to their apartment to make a sandwich. At first, he didn't touch anything but food, but the same man came back a second time to take everything else:

Pretty cold blooded, isn't it? He left the peanut butter, jelly— all the shit—out and didn't steal nothing. Ain't this about a motherfucking bitch. But then he came back again and took everything but the couches and beds. The pillows, clothes, silverware—everything. We were fucking fucked.

Eminem

The lyrics to the Mockingbird song recall the event. Apparently, Kim had also started saving some money for her daughter's college and it all vanished in one second.

Because of some of his absences, Eminem was fired from Gilbert's Lodge in December 1996, which left him with no financial means. Feelings of deep desperation started to invade his mind. What would he do? He was unable to buy diapers for his own daughter, let alone a present for Christmas. Kim saw him as a loser, because as a man, he was supposed to support his family. She then took Hailie and left him.

In this time of deep sorrow, Eminem was submerged by feelings of weakness, failure and desperation. The flop of the Infinite album added to it.

Sadness is known to be the poet's muse. In that particular night, Eminem wrote the sublime Rock Bottom song, in which he humbles himself down.

Rock Bottom can also be viewed as a philosophical reflection about the human condition.

The overwhelming feelings of helplessness and depression urged Eminem to attempt suicide. Just after he had finished writing

Rock Bottom, he took a bunch of Tylenol pills. Although the pills badly hurt his stomach, Marshall was lucky enough to survive his suicide attempt.

> *Right before I got my record deal, I was like 'I'm 23 years old, I'm not going to get a record deal, shit is not going to work out for me. I was in the studio one night and swallowed a bunch of pills and I was like 'yo, I gotta go to the hospital', but I threw up this shit out of my stomach before I had to get my stomach pumped. I threw up all over my man's basement studio. I was trying to do vocals to a song that is on my album now.*

The song mentioned above is, of course, "Rock Bottom".

Hopeless, Eminem came to suicidal thoughts:

> *I'll tell you why I took a bunch of pills on purpose. There was a record label that was stringing us along for sixth months, telling us they wanted to sign me…I found out that that dude worked in the mailroom for the label…that same night I thought I was going to die for real. When that shit happened my body was numb. I wasn't even thinking…I had my fucking face in the toilet, saying I'm going to die! I'm probably going to die…fuck it. But my body was numb from the Tylenol and I didn't really feel it. My head was spinning. I remember the room looked like going in circles. I was really fucked up. I was scared to tell my girl what happened, I told her I just got sick and was drunk at the studio.*
>
> *My boys looked out for me; they tried to keep my head up the next day, because I was still depressed. We was all depressed because FBT had a lot of money invested in me and they didn't know if they were going to make their money back, so they were depressed.*
>
> *But they were trying to keep my head up, because they knew what I was going through. I had no job; I couldn't buy my daughter diapers. It was just a fucked up time.*

One of life's most important lessons is probably never to give up hope. As dark as the present circumstances might seem, things can change in a heartbeat.

A few weeks later, Dr. Dre decided to sign Eminem to his label, which saved his life-literally:

> *The funny thing is, less than a month later, Dre called us and shit was all good, you know what I'm saying? (Eminem)*

Besides his conflicted relationship with Kim, who refused to let Eminem see his daughter for some time, the young emcee also suffered from the curse of a hostile stepfather who once pulled out a gun at his face and barked at him like an enraged dog:

> *You are no good. I don't wanna see you again or I'll kill you!*

Evict Eminem from his daughter's life, and the clever father will use his musical creativity to get mother and daughter back in his life. Not in a conventional way, though.

The "Bonnie And Clyde" song was originally meant to be a public retaliation towards Kim's behavior. In the original song, that has no boundaries in terms of violence and scary verbal imagery. Eminem uses Hailie's voice at the very tender age of two and a half.

People who are really into Eminem's music perfectly know that you often have to read the artist between the lines. The double fictional murder of Kim, which happened twice in Bonnie and Clyde and in the Kim song as well, reflects a hidden message that could be summarized by: *"Baby come back to me, I love you!"*

In his "Angry Blonde" book, Marshall Mathers clarified all the shocking details that go with some of his songs.

Love carries very multiple faces. Eminem's way of expressing it is just an unconventional way of doing it.

Eminem's best friend, D12's Proof defined the Eminem-Kim relationship the following way:

There are many wonderful things to say about Kim. People only see one side. Couples have fights, but people don't know what conversation happen in their bedrooms. Em loves his family.

One must also consider that things haven't been really simple from Kim's side when her husband became famous. Which girl would enjoy sharing her husband or boyfriend with the world?

Feeling demeaned in Eminem's songs, constantly put under the microscope by annoying teenage groupies who judged her physical appearance and way of acting. Kim felt humiliated. She probably lacked confidence too. Kim didn't ask to be featured on newspapers and magazines, she was just longing for a normal family life with daughter and husband.

On June 14, 1999, Eminem married his high school sweetheart Kim, but one year later he would file for divorce, because he saw another man kissing his wife. If Eminem wasn't particularly looking for trouble at this period of his life, trouble found him in the person of John Guerra.

John Guerra was caught kissing Kim in the parking lot of Hot Rocks Café. This kiss is described as *rather intimate*, which explains why Marshall reacted so badly, pointing an unloaded gun at his rival and promising him certain death.

John Guerra, who also happens to be a family man, really feared for his life that day. He portrays this moment as the "scariest of his life".

One moment: if John Guerra pretends to be a caring family man, why endanger himself that way, kissing another man's wife?

Kim defended herself by saying that the kiss was *"innocent"* (who is going to believe her?), but John Guerra stated quite the opposite.

Both Eminem and Kim were arrested. The charge against Kim was "disturbing the peace".

"The Kiss" is a spoken part on *The Eminem Show* CD. It recalls the painful event, in which Eminem rides with a friend who is trying to prevent him from acting crazy. Eminem then jokes about the fact that the gun is unloaded.

With her life being constantly exposed to the public; being the target of Eminem's female fans' hatred, Kim gave her own story of the event in an open letter published in the *Detroit Free Press*:

> *To whom it may concern.*
>
> *First and foremost, I would like to start off by saying that just because my husband is an entertainer, that does not mean that our personal business is for everyone's entertainment purposes, but since the press seems to think that it is, they should get their story straight.*
>
> *My husband came up to Hot Rocks Café to check up on me. Why, is still unknown to me, because if I was to cheat on him it wouldn't be in a neighborhood bar where he knows I am. Had he asked me questions before he flew off the handle, he would have realized that everyone with me (both male and female) were only friends. The fact that he just jumped to conclusions has gotten him and myself in trouble.*
>
> *I would also like to state, since my husband has no problem trying to make me look like an unfaithful wife, that every time I find pictures of him with other women, or read in magazines that he's involved with "groupies", I don't go and show up where he is, making a huge scene and getting our faces put all over the TV and newspapers. I have always taken his word on things and stood by his side. Even after the whole situation at Hot Rocks, I tried to defend him.*
>
> *Sincerely,*
> *Kimberley Mathers*

That same day, Marshall Mathers was caught in a spiral of negative events. Crossing the path of Insane Clown Posse associate Douglas Dail, Marshall pulled his gun on him.

Eminem's quick temper could have cost him his career as an emcee. Luckily, the fact that he had no previous record and that there was no serious injury played in his favor.

Judge Viviano about whom Eminem says "He treated me like a human being;" ruled that he be sentenced to two years of probation for carrying a concealed weapon. Alcohol and drug testing was also compensatory at the request of probation officers.

Into Court

Followed by a crowd of supportive fans waiting outside and a few friends, Marshall had to face sentencing for his previous actions. The video that shows him in court reveals fear and tension, until the final verdict, then an expression of deep relief falls on his face.

In the dramatic court case; the public saw Eminem's weak sides.

The artist recognized publicly that he made some mistakes, which played in his favor.

Probably because of his evil alter ego and the scary elements contained in his lyrics, the real Marshall Mathers appeared as an enigma to prosecuting attorney Marlinga:

> *This person pretends to be an out-of-control, hate filled maniac when he's on stage, but in real life, he's polite, well spoken and respectful, totally candid and honest in his statements.*

> Carl Marlinga, Prosecuting Attorney
> BBC Entertainment, April 11, 2001

Carl Marlinga is probably not the only person to be confused about Eminem. Is it really so hard to look at his real side?

Why can't he be considered just as an actor, like Larry Hagman playing the role of evil J.R. Ewing in Dallas, for instance?

Because of his wicked rhymes, a lot of people actually believe that Eminem is a bad (and negative) person in real life.

Judge Viviano's ruling was quite fair towards the artist and it allowed Eminem to consider where his mistakes lay and to amend himself.

> *I am sentencing the defendant to two years of probation on the following special conditions. The defendant has to refrain from his excessive use of alcohol and any controlled substances unless they have been especially prescribed to the defendant by a doctor.*

> *The defendant shall have no contact with John Guerra during probation and shall not engage in insulting behavior. This offence is at an end. I do not think this is a lark or a slap on the wrist. If you come back before this court, you could be sentenced to five years. I do consider any violation of probation as extremely serious.*

Eminem took the sentence seriously and tried to focus more on his artistic creativity, avoiding any kind of personal trouble.

Kim's $10 Million lawsuit and her suicide attempt

> *Every day I wake up, another drama? It's a wonder I'm alive surviving this karma*
> *If I can hold onto my private life for five minutes longer I might let my wife go with this knife*
> *Just got a feud in some parking lot with a dude over Kim and she just slit her wrists over this shit*
>   (Eminem on the "Don't Approach Me" song in
>   collaboration with Xzibit, Restless album)

The "Kim" song was too much for Kim to bear. She became deeply depressed.

Eminem was indeed beating up a naked doll he called "Kim" in front of a bunch of enthusiastic fans. This seemed more than Kim could handle.

Whatever some female Eminem fans might say, if a song explicitly talks about you and demeans you; I don't think they'd take it with humor.

How could you separate the entertainer from the real man when you happen to be married to him? It certainly wasn't simple to be in Kim's shoes during that period.

In July 2000, during the "Up In Smoke Tour"*, Kim attempted suicide in front of her mother and Eminem's little brother Nate as a reaction to this.

When her mom saw she was trying to slit her wrists with a razor blade, she immediately called an ambulance. Kim was later treated at the hospital.

One must consider that neither Eminem nor his wife was prepared to experience the nosey intrusion of the media into their lives. Neither of the two originated from the glamour world of Hollywood and this kind of exposure probably caused even more damage to the couple than the facts themselves.

Kim began seeking 10 Million dollars compensation for defamation because of the "Kim" song.

She felt that her name had been trashed in public by her famous husband.

But, Kim began showing even more signs of instability after her suicide attempt. After visiting a Detroit club, she got involved in a fight with her twin sister Dawn (Alaina's mom). The Detroit police charged her for hitting her sister in the head and the face. Kim went so far as to push her out of the limousine on the way back to Detroit from a Windsor club.

Totally destabilized, Kim also developed a drug dependency to cocaine. In 2001, she was caught in the suburbs of Harrison Township in possession of 25 grams of cocaine. The police found it at the backseat of her car. As a consequence, she was arrested, fined and eventually released after paying $3000 bail.

Drama after drama; Kim didn't seem to get a real peace of mind. Her divorce was finalized in March 2001 after a reconciliation attempt on both parties that didn't work out.

Despite their separation, Marshall and Kim have always been seeing each other. The closeness of their relationship, despite the numerous disputes and break ups, remains a mystery.

* *News Channel 2000. Com*: "911" tape released from suicide attempt of Eminem's wife.

In January 2006, Kim remarried Marshall. However their short-lived marriage lasted only four months. On April 5, 2006, just a few days before Proof's horrific murder at the CCC Club in 7 Mile, Marshall filed for divorce-once again.

If the "Kim" song became symbolic of domestic violence and misogyny, it should nevertheless be regarded by the neutral listener as nothing else but a horror tale in which Eminem is incarnating a betrayed man and a psychopathic killer. There is no difference between listening to the Kim song and watching a thriller on TV. It is all fictional. The listener must acknowledge that this is not the real Marshall Mathers acting in real life, but his made stage character unleashing his fictional anger.

Eminem has often been described in the media as a vile person, a monster and a violent misogynist. His lyrics have even been used —intentionally—in women's course studies to demonstrate how bad Eminem's music was for the reflection of women's images in young men's minds. A few people also went so far as to call him a *"women beater"*.

Yes, Eminem does have misogynistic sounding lyrics. True, he has "murdered" Kim several times in his songs. Everything is pure fiction, but the anger expressed in his songs is real and refers to real facts.

Eminem never ever harmed Kim in real life. It was well known, from eye-witnesses such as Dan Carlisle aka MC Hush and Bob Claus that Kim was the dominating and manipulating element in the couple.

Mc Hush and Eminem used to be neighbors. They lived between Nowara and Bentler Street in Detroit. They were friends and also close collaborators. As insiders of the Detroit hip hop scene would probably know, Hush is the co-founder of the Da Ruckus group along with Jermaine Harbin aka Uncle ILL. All three emcees collaborated on the well-known Eminem song "We Shine". MC Hush also happens to be the producer to the beats of the mischievous "Slim Shady" EP.

Consider MC Hush as a key person in witnessing Eminem's rocky relationship with Kim. MC Hush confirmed, *"Everything Eminem says in his lyrics is true."*

Dan Carslisle and Marshall Mathers knew each other very well. He was very much aware of Eminem's struggle to provide his family with a comfortable life. He perfectly understood Eminem's state of mind after the flop of his *Infinite* album:

> *By the summer of '95, Em was like 'Man, I got a baby on the way. I gotta do something. I gotta make money somewhere or there is no way I can take care of this shit. He just seemed overwhelmed. I remember a few months before our babies were due riding together to do a cable TV show. He didn't even want to go. I was like 'you got to promote your shit', but he was just angry. He'd put out on Infinite and it wasn't doing well. Rap radio wasn't really wild about playing a record by a white kid. Everybody was talking that Vanilla Ice shit. When radio DJ Billy T did finally play it, he actually faded it out just when Em's verse came up. He was crushed. He was like' Man, if this record doesn't hit, this is it, I quit. (Mc Hush)*

Both their kids were born at the same time. Mc Hush recalls his friend Marshall's huge financial difficulties and his struggles in finding a stable job:

> *Hailie was born on Christmas day…my son was born right before that. But Em wasn't living with Kim because he had to get his act together. He had a car, this beat up Mercury tracer*

and he'd get a job, making pizzas, cooking, whatever he'd got from one job to another. But he just didn't have the money, so Hailie had to live with Kim and her parents on the east side.

In addition to Marshall's difficulties in trying to make a living for his family, Kim would show her shady face on several occasions. Her manipulative character would surface and Hailie would be caught in the middle of the couple's arguments:

Sometimes, he'd have Hailie for the day over at the house on Novara. Kim would just show up and grab Hailie and he'd be like "You bitch!" She was always holding stuff over his head for him to see the baby, like spending more time with her instead of his friends. He kept on saying he was gonna kill her ass. That's what's the song Bonnie and Clyde came from.

To the people who have approached her, Kim is known as a woman of strong character. In fact, it wasn't Marshall who showed violent behavior towards her: in fact, Kim slapped her ex-husband a lot during arguments:

He and Kim had to fight like once a day; it was a mandatory thing. Always in the kitchen. I'd hear her smacking him and no matter what, he wouldn't hit her back. I hate to say it, but she kicked the shit out of him. He would never hit her. But she's a manly chick. When they were in a fight, he'd scream a little but back down. There was something in him afraid of her, enough to let her win all the time. He was afraid she wouldn't let him see his daughter.

Some might call Marshall a coward and a weak person because of his attitude in front of Kim. I call it fatherly love. Because he wanted his relationship to his daughter to be kept safe, Eminem didn't mind looking like a loser in front of his ex-wife and friends.

Watching a few situations from Kim's point of views, Eminem's fame certainly affected their relationship later on. It is fully understandable. Being married to a famous person is far from being a fairy tale. It is closer to a living nightmare, when you consider that nearly everybody wants a piece of Eminem, which barely leaves time for a real relationship.

On the other hand, and long before Eminem became the superstar he is now, Kim put Marshall into some very embarrassing situation.

The Hot Rock café incident is just one of them.

Back in 1997, Kim had taken a job in the Oasis Executive SPA on Van Dike Center line. This is a massage parlor, at first glance, a normal job. The parlor was engaged in the prostitution business, though.

Debbie. Eminem's mom first tried to hide what Kim's job was about the best she could. She then gave a call to MC Hush:

> *His mom called me up one day and she was like' you gotta go get Marshall because he's gonna kill her.*

Kim's unusual job drove Marshall mad when he knew about it. She had to stop it. Kim is a clever manipulator and Marshall often appears as her victim in their love life.

As the product from a dysfunctional background, Marshall nevertheless appears to be the stable element of his family. As far as we can look into the past stories, he always fought to provide his family some stability.

His demeaning lyrics against Kim are the expression of an unhappy love. They are like an urgent wake up call for Kim to realize what she is doing to him.

Slim Shady might be a scary character, but Kim often revealed her shady face in public.

In 2006, Kim spoke out about her volatile relationship with her husband on *Mojo In The Morning* and took part in the "Single Mingles" event organized by the same Detroit radio station.

Kim has also talked publicly about her arguments with her former husband on the Dr. Keith Ablow show, in 2007, and it has been recently rumored (April 2012) that Kim Mathers would take part in a TV Reality show entitled *Motor City Wives*. No official confirmation has been given, though.

The Only Lady He Adores: Hailie

If she had never been born, I would have nothing around me to make me truly happy. (Eminem)

Maybe it is about time some star struck people stopped putting their idols on a pedestal and stopped considering them as extraterrestrials. Eminem could make a trillion dollars a year; he would still be a human being, facing the same problems random persons would face in their daily lives. Eminem is no different: he is a regular person, a family man, who, (stardom aside), leads a quiet, normal life with his daughter.

Like all of us, he has weaknesses. Far from being the monster and pervert some hostile media made him look like, he is a normal person, whose wicked lyrics are so often taken out of their original context.

Hailie Jade Scott's birth radically changed Eminem's perception of life. Being a father gave the artist a new sense of responsibility; somebody to cherish and to care for:

You know, my little girl was the real wake up call for me. She made me get my ass in gear to make something out of my life and try ten quadrillion times harder than I had before.

While it might appear as contradictory to a bunch of people how the rapper with the most wicked lyrics heard all around the world could possibly be a good father; one has to keep in mind that, "before being Eminem; he is a father" (to quote Eminem)

Maybe Eminem has chosen a liberal attitude towards education. But he remains a responsible father in any case:

I gotta get up, thank God I got a little girl and I'm a responsible father.

Eminem's dysfunctional and fatherless past deeply scarred him. As a kid, he was looking for affection, a father figure and security. These are elements that were absent in his past. Therefore, Marshall Mathers had to provide his daughter with a secure environment in which he has played a major role.

He fought for years to achieve something in the field he was the most gifted for; that was rap music, and mainly because of little Hailie.

In *Saying Goodbye To Hollywood*, Eminem states:

All I wanted was to give Hailie the life I never had.

Hailie is often described in his songs as the only true reason to live for. All the money Eminem has made as a rapper and the clever businessman he has become; is for his daughter. Of course, he wants her to attend college.

When he is staying at home, Eminem is a pretty normal father. The day's routine is what you'd expect in any average American family, no special fantasy—just a random father spending time with his little daughter:

> *When I'm home, I wake her up in the morning, I feed her some cereal, watch a little TV, take her to school and pick her up. Lately, I've been taking her to the studio, because that's where I spend most of my time. She has fun there; there's video games for her and stuff. Coloring books and crayons—thank God for those. We watch a lot of movies, just typical shit. She's really into the Powerpuff Girls and Hey Arnold! And Dora the Explorer—ever seen that one? It's the same episode all week long because it teaches kids numbers and how to speak Spanish. By Friday, you know it by heart. I watch that with her; then I go listen to my songs over and over. I'm gonna fucking jump off the bridge.*

Despite the numerous arguments that might have separated them as a couple, Eminem and Kim always tried to instill their daughter with the best values they could. According to his own statements, Eminem always bent his knees with his daughter to pray with her when he was at home.

Of course, Hailie had to face some real difficult situations during her childhood. Her mother went AWOL in 2003 after violating her probation. She also suffered a lot from her father's absence and probably his drug addiction too. But given the circumstances, she had a fairly normal life, thanks to her caring dad.

Hailie's features on Eminem's CD have often been misinterpreted. They have often been viewed as the rapper's commercial exploitation of his own child.

When he put his daughter on his records, his intentions were totally different. First of all, the emcee wanted his daughter to be part of his work.

Hailie Jade's role in Eminem's music through the years

The making of a little star:

I want her to be able to grow up and look back on this and be like, whether people agree with it or not, "My dad put me on a song. My dad wrote songs for me; my dad said my name all over the place." I want her to be able to look back in magazines and everything and just know. I don't ever wanna be like my father was to me.

Eminem

Hailie on '97 Bonnie and Clyde

Back when Marshall was fighting with Kim. When their relationship was off, Kim didn't allow Marshall to see his daughter. Hailie had become a bad weapon against Marshall.

I remember watching an old video from 1998 where you saw a younger Eminem wearing some glasses telling people about the release of the *Slim Shady* LP. While announcing his future release he kept saying, while flipping the bird: « *I will talk about my baby's mama. This is some real shit* ».

Of course, he was referring to the '97 "Bonnie and Clyde" song. Not only was this a misinterpreted song in which a two-year-old Hailie ended up as her dad's accomplice in her mom's murder and reconciliation attempt with Kim, but also it was also rich with a very touching message:

> *Baby, your dada loves you (hey)*
> *And I'ma always be here for you (hey)*
> *No matter what happens*
> *You're all I got in this world*
> *I would never give you up for nothin'*
> *Nobody in this world is ever gonna keep you from me*
> *I love you…*

The '97 "Bonnie and Clyde" song introduces Hailie to the world. Little Hailie chatters in the background and has become a hip-hop heroine, a gangsta character. Despite its scary background, the "Bonnie and Clyde" song is a beautiful treasure of fatherly love and devotion.

Eminem's first ode to Hailie: "Hailie's Song"

Several years later, after releasing his controversial Marshall Mathers LP, Eminem was back with a brand new and explosive CD: *The Eminem Show*. The CD offered a critical view and some insight about American society and politics.

I was mixed up with some funny and dramatic elements. In the middle of all those typical Eminem songs, "Hailie's Song", is a touching ode from a daddy to his daughter.

When I bought *The Eminem Show* in 2002, "Hailie's Song" was the song that I discovered just after White America.

Some critics accused Eminem of « turning pop » because of this beautiful song of his, but I think I understood his intentions quite immediately. Eminem merely wanted to show his audience that he was also capable of singing songs besides his rapping abilities. "Hailie's Song" is deep and touching. The song is a sweet combination of soft violin notes and real feelings put on paper.

"Hailie's Song" shows a daddy's gratitude towards his daughter's presence in his life.

Hailie in My Dad's Gone Crazy

The last song of *The Eminem Show* is written like a comedy, a funny daddy-daughter dialogue in which Eminem acts crazy and Hailie comes to rescue her dad.

The listener should pay attention to Eminem's words:

> *My songs can make you cry, take you by surprise*
> *And at the same time, make you dry your eyes with the same rhyme*

While playing the fool with Hailie, Eminem talks about serious subjects and pours his heart out about the drama of September 11th and his beloved Uncle Ronnie's death.

Hailie fires back in Doe Rae Me

> *My daughter is the closest thing to my heart. You say something about my daughter, then there's no boundaries; everything is open, and Hailie might come on the record and diss you, too. So don't fuck with me when it comes to my daughter.*

Eminem, *Rolling Stone Interview,* June 2004)

Four rappers have dissed Hailie in her songs: Everlast, Esham, Ja Rule and Benzino. If « personals » are part of the rap game, I do consider that they should be aimed at the rapper himself, not at their child.

If you talk bad about one of my sons, I might kill you. A parent is driven mad when you attack his or her kid. It is a mean and cowardly way of rapping, as far as I am concerned.

Eminem is more clever than most of his opponents. Ja Rule and Benzino put Hailie on a song, dissing her badly. Ok, guys, you put Eminem's daughter on a record? Guess what, Hailie is gonna respond to your attacks and make you look ridiculous!

That's exactly what Hailie did!

Eminem, Obie Trice and D12 might have assisted the little girl, but her dialogue is killing Ja Rule:

> *[Hailie] Daddy is Ja Rule taller than me?*
>
> *Eminem] No honey you guys are the same size.*
> *Eminem, Do Rae Me*

If you want to mess with Eminem, don't touch his daughter or you might regret it. Marshall doesn't play with his feelings for his daughter. Hailie is the closest person to his heart.

Mockingbird: second ode to Hailie

Maybe the greatest gift Eminem has ever offered to his fans is his "Mockingbird" video. In that wonderful and touching video, Eminem went over the top to invite us into his living room. He didn't choose actors to play Hailie, Alaina or Kim. He simply took a real former video featuring his loved ones.

This video is an open dialogue with Hailie during which Marshall is trying to explain his own failures and Kim's whereabouts.

The video allows people to picture every-day life scenes at Eminem's home. Touching, deep and refreshing scenes of little Hailie's life allow people to understand the daddy—daughter relationship better.

When I'm Gone: Hailie reuniting her parents

Eminem's song and video are full of pain and "When I'm Gone" sounds like an apology to Hailie.

Very sincere and conscious of his addiction problems, Eminem depicts scenes of conflict with his daughter. Hailie suffers from his absence and sometimes wouldn't let her father go.

Following her daddy like an angel in her thoughts and prayers, Hailie makes her dad realize that his place is at home with his family.

Since the beginning of his career, Hailie has played different roles in his music. Accomplice in crime, weapon between her parents' struggles, Ja Rule's opponent, daddy's little angel, a little girl in pain.

Eminem has been criticized for putting his daughter in his songs. I find it wonderful that a rapper like him with some incisive and wicked lyrics showed his soft side to his public. He managed to transform this love and dedication toward his daughter into beautiful music notes pleasing to many fans' ears.

In his 2010 interview with Tanya Simon on CBS, Eminem expressed about parenting. To put things clear, the rapper pointed out that he doesn't cuss at home in front of his daughters:

> *I'm a parent. I have daughters. I mean, how would I really sound, as a person…walking around my house, saying 'Bitch, pick this up,' you know what I mean?*

> *I don't cuss.*

Eminem doesn't feel responsibility towards the youth for the profanity contained in his lyrics. He considers that parents have to educate their kids the right way.

> *I feel like it's your job to parent them. If you're the parent, be a parent.*

Eminem's music made Hailie very popular. A lot of new Hailie pictures, showing a 16-year-old teenage girl have been leaked on the Internet.

On a side note, some impersonators are often trying to take advantage of the young teenage girl's popularity. This is how *E! Online* reported a fake Twitter account entitled "Angry Blonde" in which the shameless poser had the nerve to tweet to "Kim Mathers" and to "Chris Brown". The account was also fully loaded with fake Hailie pictures. The incident goes back to 2011. Identity theft should be severely punished.

Nathan Mathers

Nate Kane Samra Mathers is Eminem's half brother. He was born to Debbie in February 1986.

Nathan experienced a similar childhood to Marhall's. He was bullied at school as one of the only white kids around.

Marshall pretty much raised his little brother who now lives with him. Nathan even accompanied his bother while touring and is featured on several videos like *The Way I Am*, *Sing For The Moment* and *Without Me*.

Although his relationship to his mom might have been complicated, Nathan doesn't share his brother's strong feelings about his mom. He stated publicly that he loves her.

Nathan has also embraced a rapping career since 2006.

He is working with a skilled young local rapper and friend called Zack Groulx, better known to the insiders as MC Solystic.

The young man is, of course, not as experienced as his brother, but he managed to show some interesting skills. One of Nate's main assets is probably his vocals. Nate's voice is set on a darker register than his brothers', which will allow him to make a real difference.

In "The Shadow Of A Celebrity" song, being Eminem's brother doesn't have advantages, particularly when your ambition is to become an emcee too.

You don't want to be looked at as your brother's carbon copy, but people will make comparisons quite automatically.

A hip-hop giant like Eminem would outshine most beginners.

At some point, it must have been hard for Nathan to realize that some shameless groupies must have been using him to get at his famous brother.

If you are curious to know more about Nathan Mathers' music and biography, check his personal website: www.reverbnation. com/natekane

Todd Nelson

It never occurs to me that he's famous. I changed his diapers when he was a kid.

Todd Nelson

Todd Nelson is Debbie's younger brother and, thus Marshall's uncle.

Eminem spent a few years at uncle Todd's house in the early 80's in Warren, in a little house, that became famous thanks to Eminem's "Marshall Mathers" LP CD cover.

The two-family home was in the family for several generations. Eminem's great grandmother, Bessi Viola Whitacker had bought it in 1950.

Because of financial problems that were too heavy to bear for Todd, the home was put on sale on Ebay in 2002:

This is a very emotional thing for me, because this house has been in our family for 50 years. I didn't want to sell it, but I had to because my finances won't allow me to live here anymore.

Todd is an important witness of Eminem's childhood and teenage years. He helped raise Marshall who lived on and off at his house while attending Lincoln High School.

However, Todd Nelson was absent from his nephew's life from 1992 to 1998, serving a jail sentence for manslaughter in a case of self-defense.

The relationship between nephew and uncle seemed to be cool in the beginning. As he stated it in the Eminem aka DVD that contains some precious material related to Eminem's roots and childhood, Todd used to go fishing with his nephew and teach him about life. At some point, he probably compensated for Marshall's father's absence.

But the whirlwind of Eminem's fame seemed to have devastated it all.

An insider of this period who was befriended by Todd (who won't be named to protect his privacy); told me that Marshall's fame had made Todd quite bitter. As a matter of fact, uncle and nephew did not seem to keep in touch very frequently.

Todd tried to sell some of his nephew's past pictures and drawings over the net. One can only question what his real motives were when he was trying to give his nephew a bad name. It appears that he didn't really seem very supportive of his nephew at all when he reached the top. The closeness of his relationship to his sister Debbie probably has to do with it.

Todd would stick up for Debbie no matter what, regardless of a misrepresentation of the truth and some contradictory statements emerging from different members of Eminem's family.

In a detailed, unbiased article that was published in *Metro Times** on October 30, 2002, entitled The Real Slim Shady, the journalist Hobey Echlin analysed different elements of Eminem's past in regard with some witnesses' statements.

This thorough analysis is truly interesting, because it envisions Marshall Mathers from each camp's perspectives, which allows the reader to make up his own opinion without being influenced one way of another.

It appears that Todd actually held his music and friends responsible for becoming 'a bad person.' It is also interesting to know that Todd didn't back Eminem's rough childhood memories, nor the facts related in his movie, "8 Mile". Todd, who once publicly stated that *'he loved Marshall a lot'*, went as far as calling his nephew a 'fake':

> *He's my nephew, but I call him my 'F.U.' I don't like fake people. His movie shouldn't be called "8 Mile" — it should be called '26 Mile'!*

Moreover, Todd would also portray his nephew as a racist, mom-loving son with an Oedipus complex:

> *Every white male regardless of his age has something against their mother, and he's exploiting that, so all these white males can throw themselves a pity party. He tried bashing blacks and fags and when that didn't work he started bashing his mother.*

Todd Nelson's arguments don't really sound convincing. If it was only about bashing his mom, Eminem could have found lots of other persons in the world to diss on a record. The rap game allows you to diss anybody you want, and preferably fellow emcees.

Moreover, some other eyewitnesses that are not family members seem to have confirmed Eminem's version. Growing up with a single mother on welfare must have been rough in any case.

Even if we assume that some facts might have been exaggerated a little bit, the facts tend to prove that Debbie's Munchhausen's syndrome, her temper tantrums and her troubled personality were quite real (as stated in the "Cleaning Out My Closet" song).

In another attempt to justify Debbie's upbringing of her son Marshall, Todd would also describe his sister as a person 'under constant pressure' 'who was doing her best to raise her son'*

> *His dad Bruce made wood veneer, you know, that they put on tables. They were married, but he moved to South Dakota. Debbie had nowhere to go. Her dad rejected her. She could've stayed there in St. Joe, where Marshall would've had no chance — people pick up aluminum cans and sell bait down there. But she decided to do it alone, and brought Marshall*

up North. She was overwhelmed. I remember her standing in the doorway of our mother's house. I was like, 'What are you gonna do? Come in or stay out.' It was the wintertime, and she had that look in her eyes — she was so lost. (Todd Nelson)

As a matter of fact, Debbie's first intentions about her son must have been good. Moving to Detroit was giving Marshall more interesting future job perspectives than staying in a middle working class town like Saint Joseph, Missouri. Being a single mother struggling to raise two kids can be a harsh struggle. Any single mom would confirm that the fight is not only about feeding your kids and paying your bills, but also much more about raising your children right and giving them good values for their future.

Whatever people might think, Debbie probably did her best to raise Marshall. But it doesn't mean she did the right thing, accordingly to her boy's needs. Her troubled personality, the outside difficulties she must have been facing, her drug addiction, her numerous boyfriends, all these elements weighed heavily on the negative balance. If we look at it carefully, all that was very destabilizing for Debbie's little boy.

One could wonder where Todd got all the inside info about his nephew, as he used to display it in British tabloids quite frequently. Kim's bisexuality was exposed publicly by Todd who didn't shy away from giving crusty details to the press about Eminem's threesomes with his ex-wife.

Why did Todd want to sell any private info about his nephew to the British tabloids? Was he bitter because he thought Marshall should have supported him financially?

Did he want some publicity from the media? Or did he simply want to set the record straight about some of Marshall's statements he fully disagreed with?

The truth, as always, probably lies in the middle.

Another suicide case in the Mathers family

On October 19, 2004, a few weeks before of Eminem's Encore CD release, Todd Nelson's life would end tragically. Eminem's uncle, who was depressed about an unresolved situation, shot himself in the head.

The cause of his suicide was a sheriff's Rottweiler dog that happened to scare his family. According to numerous reports, Todd couldn't cope with it any more.

> *Todd had been very upset about a Rottweiler owned by a local sheriff who was causing problems for his family. The dog scared his girlfriend's son and scratched his car. But when he complained to police, they wouldn't do anything about it.*
>
> *He shot himself in his car in his own backyard. My grandson, Todd Jr. found his body. He thought his dad was asleep but he was dead. He called me and then Marshall and the rest of the family.*
>
> Betty Kresin

Although Eminem didn't attend Todd's funeral, he paid for the ceremony that took place in Saint Joseph, Missouri.

The news of his uncle's suicide must have been hard to cope with. It probably resurfaced a lot of older memories about Ronnie's suicide in 1991. A family friend expressed about it:

> *This news has hit Marshall hard. It will bring back all the memories of losing Ronnie. To lose two uncles at such a young age is terribly sad, especially as his father has never been around. The fact they both committed suicide is so tragic.*

An EMINEM Photo Tour

White Kid in a Black Music World

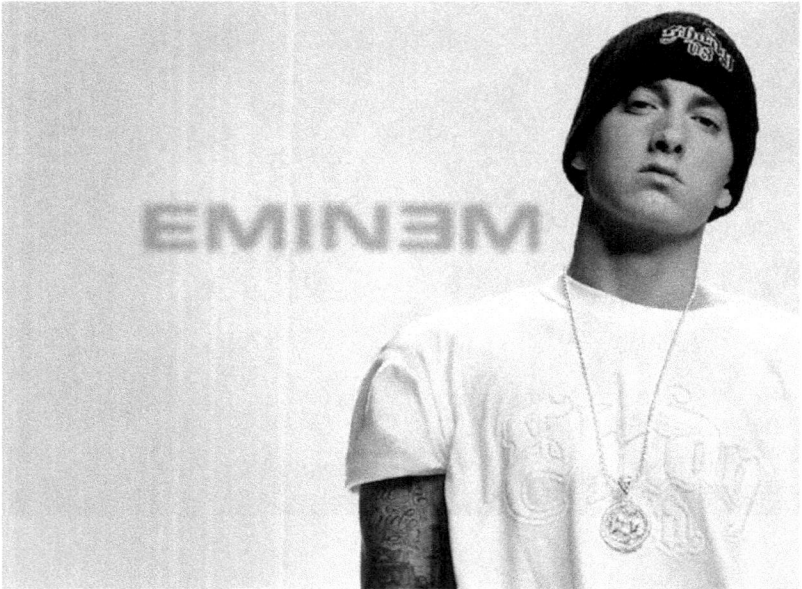

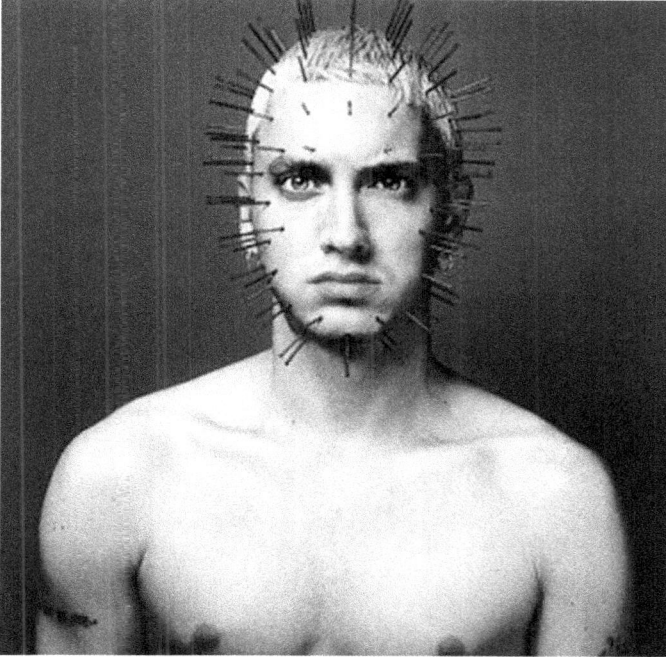

Chapter 5:

"8 Mile", Eminem's Movie

Marshall Mathers' semi autobiographical movie, "8 Mile" opened the world of hip-hop to many neophytes. It also helped to do away with many misconceptions about the artist's upbringing and environment.

It raised a lot of passion (and sometimes controversy—because of its strong language. The use of drugs and alcohol added to it—of course).

Eminem's interpretation of Jimmy Smith Jr. was fresh, natural and very close to reality. The viewer was able to transport himself into the Detroit environment of the mid-90s and to slip into the skin of a white emcee struggling for recognition with a black audience.

The atmosphere of the hip-hop scene was reproduced with a great dose of realism. No Hollywood bubble gum world, but the reality in all its roughness. A working class hero was pictured on his road to success. The concept was new and excellent, because a thirsty public was in need of authenticity.

Why is Eminem's movie called "8 Mile"?

"8 Mile" refers to 8 Mile Road in Detroit, the border between the black neighborhood (7 Mile Road) and the white neighborhood (9 Mile Road). The border, which is real, also refers to a psychological border that separates two different communities and cultures.

"8 Mile" is also the border that separates us from reality (the problems we may face, our current standard of living) and the place where we want to be, our dream coming true. Everybody can relate to that border, because it exists and might be latent in us. We all have dreams we'd like to catch.

The "313" is an area code that refers to the Detroit hood.

Although some details of Eminem's life have been purposely modified in "8 Mile", the movie allows the viewer to catch a glimpse of the Detroit hip-hop scene.

One of the first scenes puts the camera on Jimmy's terrified face: stage fright literally paralyzed the young emcee who stood mute in front of his opponent.

Starring as Jimmy Smith Jr., a young aspiring rapper, Eminem tells the story of a white emcee who expresses his anger and frustrations through his music as well as his daily life with his mother (played by Kim Basinger), in a trailer park.

Jimmy aka Bunny Rabbit lives there with his mom's boyfriend (Michael Shannon), a former school buddy who is nearly the same age as him, and his little sister Lily (Chloe Greenfield).

Jimmy works hard at Detroit Stamping, an automotive factory, doing overtime, in order to save some money for his own studio. During the weekend Jimmy attends live mic sessions at the Hip Hop Shop. The underground emcee fight on two fronts: proving his rapping skills and trying to offer some stability to his little sister who is stuck in the trailer park with an alcoholic mom.

Jimmy finds his solace in writing lyrics and rapping. Jimmy's love interest, a young girl named Alex is brilliantly interpreted by Brittany Murphy. Caught between passion and betrayal, the temptation of "easy music industry connections" through Wink, Jimmy Smith aka Bunny Rabbit eventually gains some recognition on the local scene after winning three battles, highly encouraged by Future (Mekhi Pfifer), a true friend who hosts local shows.

Since his rapping debut, Eminem has always been reproached for his angry attitude. After watching the movie, Eminem's environment and living conditions will be clarified to many viewers.

The movie is vibrant, full of passion and puts hip-hop in a favorable light.

Eminem's musical work had already won the public's approval since 1999, but Marshall Mathers had yet to prove that he could act. His authentic and natural play in front of the camera is undeniable. The Jimmy Smith character symbolizes the harsh struggle of Detroit's working classes. It is fulfilled with a good dose of anger, uncertainties and courage.

The emcee sacrifices his present for a better future, thanks to his lyrical skills.

The three 8 Mile battles

Three battles at the end of the 8 Mile movie made Jimmy Smith aka B. Rabbit a reputation in the rap arena: a real challenge for Jimmy Smith who had stage fright.

People who are not into hip-hop need to realize the importance of a rap battle; rap battles can be compared to battles we have to face in real life.

Words used in a freestyle or a rap battle are like a sword, they expose your opponent to total nudity. When you get verbally ripped off, it is your turn to show your teeth and to use your verbal weapons in order to weaken your adversary. It's a matter of honor, you have to expose and verbally annihilate your enemy in order to make him look bad or ridiculous in front of a crowd that expects your answer with impatience. You can feel this kind of fever in "8 Mile" when the crowd shouts: *"What? What?"* which means that it is your turn to respond.

Eminem perfectly knows the importance of a battle:

> *That's one thing that I want this movie to get across, is that people who live in this world of hip-hop—how seriously we*

> *take this, how seriously we take our music and battling and*
> *the sport of it and the competition and everything.*

Losing a battle is terrible in an aspiring rapper's mind. Since the time he was unable to spit any word on stage, Jimmy Smith had been humiliated by Alex who had cheated on him with Wink. He had to take lyrical revenge and prove his skills, in order to keep his honor safe.

Lickety Split battles B Rabbit on the *"whiteness of his music"*. He enumerates numerous white artists like Vanilla Ice and Elvis. He wants to prove that Jimmy's music is bad rap or even worse, no rap at all. The reference to Willie Nelson who -by the way—makes country music is intended to ridicule Jimmy. The only reference to a black artist is Tina Turner in a weak position, when she gets beaten up by her husband. He also points out his mistakes and the mistakes of his friend like Cheddar Bob!

> *Yo, this guys a choke-artist*
> *Ya catch a bad one*
> *Ya better off shootin ya-self wit Popa Doc's handgun*
> *Climbin up this mountain, ya weak*
> *I leave ya lost witout a paddle, floatin shit's creek*
> *You ain't Detroit, I'm the D*
> *You tha new kid on the block, bout to get smacked back to the*
> *boone-docks*
> *F**kin Nazi, this crowd ain't ya type*
> *Take some real advice*
> *And form a group with Vanilla Ice*
> *And what I tell ya*
> *Ya better use it*
> *This guy's a hillbilly this ain't Willie Nelson music*
> *Trailer trash*
> *I choke ya till ya last breath*
> *And have ya lookin foolish like Cheddar Bob when he shot*
> *his-self*
> *Silly Rabbit, I know why they call you that*
> *Cuz you follow Future, like he got carrots up his asscrack*

> *And when you act it up, that's when you got jacked up*
> *And left stupid like Tina Turner when she got smacked up*
> *I crack ya shoulderblade*
> *You'll get dropped so hard that Elvis will start turnin in his grave*
> *I don't know why they left you out in the dark*
> *Ya need to take your white ass back across 8 Mile to the trailer*
> *Park.*

In the first battle, Bunny Rabbit battles his opponent on his sugar-coated music style that questions his masculinity and his music style that looks like it was aimed at a 100% female audience. The first sentence is hilarious:

> *This guy raps like his parents jerked him*

The great majority of a hip-hop battle audience is usually composed of men:

> *He sounds like Eric Sermon*
> *The generic version*
> *This whole crowd looks suspicious*
> *It's all dudes in here*
> *Except for these bitches*

He goes on making fun of the Free World leaders:

> *That's ok, you look like a fuckin worm with braids*
> *These leaders of the Free World rookies*
> *Lookie, how can 6 dicks be pussies*

He also makes himself look in a positive light, he enforces his role as a fighter and shoots at his enemy in a funny way.

Lickety is too slow to follow Rabbit's rapid flow:

> *Ya they call me Rabbit*
> *This is a turtle race*
> *He can't get wit me spittin this shit*
> *Wickedy Lickety shot*
> *Spicious spickety split Lickety*
> *So I'ma turn around with a great smile*
> *And walk my white ass back across 8 Mile*

Bunny Rabbit conquered the crowd. But he had to battle Lotto.

Second round. Second fight.

Like his fellow Lickety Split, Lotto comes with a strong racial argument, which appears to be a bad strategy:

> *Huhhh huhhh*
> *I'll spit a racial slur honkey sue me*
> *This shit is a horror flick*
> *But a black guy doesn't die in this movie*
> *Fuckin wit Lotto dog you gotta be kiddin*
> *That makes me believe, you really don't have an interest in livin*
> *You think these niggas gone feel the shit you say?*

His hatred of Jimmy, as a white man, clearly appears in his whole speech. Jimmy fully counters his attack in the second part of his verse:

> *Matta fact dog, here's a pencil*
> *Go home, write some shit, make it suspenseful*
> *And don't come back until somethin dope hits you*
> *Fuck it*
> *You can take the Mic home wich you*
> *Lookin like a cyclone hit you*
> *Tanktop screamin, "Lotto I don't fit you"*
> *You see how far them white jokes get you*
> *Boys like, how Vanilla Ice gone diss you?*
> *My motto:*
> *Fuck Lotto*
> *I get the 7 digits from ya mother for a dollar tomorrow*

Third and final round: Bunny Rabbit vs. Papa Doc.

Bunny Rabbit has managed to get rid of two of his enemies. He feels better about himself and has gained some confidence.

He now rallies the crowd from the 313:

> *Now everybody from the 3-1-3*
> *Put ya muthafuckin hands up and follow me*
> *Everybody from the 3-1-3*

Put ya muthafuckin hands up
Look look

People from the Detroit ghetto are proud to belong to the 313 area calling code. People from the 313 are supposed to be cool unlike the people from the 810 area.

Jimmy's strategy is intelligently worked out. He perfectly knows his worst enemy, who-by the way—doesn't raise his hand:

Now while he stands tough
Notice that this man did not have his hands up
This Free World's got ya gased up
Now who's afraid of the Big Bad Wolf

He knows that he's a gangster wannabe. There is nothing *ghetto* nor "gangsta" in him :

1, 2, 3 and to the 4
1pac, 2pac, 3pac, 4
4pac, 3pac, 2pac's, 1
Your Pac, he's Pac, No Pac's, None

But Bunny Rabbit's best strategy is his huge honesty and it will pay off in the end. He doesn't hide what he is or his mistakes:

I am white
I am a fuckin bum
I do live in the trailer wit my mom
My boy future is an Uncle Tom
I do got a dumb friend named Cheddar Bob who shoots himself
in his leg with his own gun
I did get jumped
By all 6 of you chumps
And Wink did fuck my girl
I'm still standin here screamin fuck the Free World!

Then Rabbit reveals Papa Doc's intimate and hidden secrets to the crowd:

But I know somethin about you
You went to Cranbrook, that's a private school

> *What's the matter dog you embarrassed?*
> *This guys a gangster? His real name's Clarence*
> *And Clarence lives at home with both parents*
> *And Clarence parents have a real good marriage*
> *This guy don't wanna battle, he's shook*
> *Cuz ain't no such things as Half Way Crooks!*
> *He's scared to death*
> *He's scared to look*
> *At his fuckin yearbook*
> *Fuck Cranbook*

Jimmy's great force lies in his total honesty. He is not ashamed of living in a trailer park and even proud to be "white trash":

> *Fuck a beat, I go acapella*
> *Fuck a Popa Doc, fuck a clock, fuck a trailer fuck everybody*
> *Fuck yall if you doubt me, I'ma piece of fuckin white trash I say it proudly*
> *And fuck this battle I don't wanna win, I'm outtie*
> *Here, tell these people somethin they don't know about me*

Papa Doc is left totally un-weaponed and speechless. This is a happy end for Rabbit who eventually wins his fight for recognition.

These 3 rap battles from "8 Mile" also teach us a lesson about real life: don't try to play yourself. Be honest, accept yourself with your imperfections, your failures, your mistakes, but always be yourself.

Eminem on "8 Mile"

Eminem gave some insight about his working conditions and the difficulties he faced with acting, something he was not really familiar with. Authenticity mattered a lot to Marshall and he worked very hard to reach the goal that was set to a high standard.

In his movie as well as in his music, Marshall Mathers manages to raise enthusiasm.

> *I thought when I first read the script that it was gonna be impossible for me to memorize all these lines. But the truth we did a lot of rehearsing. We did months of it. All the biggest*

scenes rehearsed off camera…Me and Mekhi, me and Brittany, everybody came together. So if it looks we're friends onscreen it's because we became friends. We had no choice but to. There were like eight hours of rehearsal a day, two months until we started shooting, just to get us warmed up. I work a lot of hours in the studio, but it's on my time and it is something I'm in control of. It hurts being on someone else's schedule and somebody else's time. It was gruesome. It was like acting boot camp. It was tough. Like 5 in the morning 'til seven, eight at night. Then get back up, literally have enough time to go to sleep, and come right back. I couldn't help but be this character in the movie.

I just wanted to be natural in the film, basically do what I would do in a situation that if I was placed in it, or what my character would do. Basically I wanted to feel real in every scene. And I felt like as long as I felt authentic it was cool.

Playing the role of Jimmy Smith Jr. required a lot of humbleness from Eminem, who had to literally go back to the period in which he was a nobody; struggling to make a name—an essential condition for him to be regarded as authentic by his audience.

This movie took me back to that time, that place, stripped me of all ego, before I was Eminem, before I was anybody. I had to go back to that. I was humbled to the point I was Jimmy Smith, Jr.; I wasn't Eminem, I was this dude who had no name and still hadn't come out of his shell yet. That's how seriously I took the film. And that's how I knew I had to write the songs for the movie during that time. Because I felt I was really in it.

In order to interpret a realistic Jimmy Smith, Eminem also had to lose a lot of weight, so he could physically incarnate the broke, underground emcee in his time of hardships.

Impressions from "8 Mile"

The positive aspect of the movie is that no matter where you come from, you can break out of that. If your mentality is right and your drive is right, you can break out of that circle. You

> *can make something of your life. The whole point of the movie is that it doesn't matter where you come from, the North Side or the South Side of 8 Mile, you can break out of it.*

Eminem

Eminem's authenticity, his great charisma, his talent in the movie won a lot of hearts. The movie has to be regarded as symbolic, as it does not recall every detail of Marshall Mathers' former life.

Whether you like rap music or not, you are transported into Eminem's world, becoming the spectator of his numerous struggles, his anxiousness and vulnerability. You will witness his creativity and lyrical ability. In the end, you will understand that this white kid was made to rap.

The Jimmy Smith character appears as a caring family man, a brother who is worried about his mom's alcohol addiction and his sister's living conditions. Jimmy is a young white guy with extraordinary rapping skills who constantly struggles for acceptance into the black community, while his efforts will barely be taken seriously. Deshaun Holton aka Proof (Lil Tic)'s freestyle at the beginning of the movie is quite symbolic of the black audience's opinion about white emcees.

With the help of his friend Future and some other fellows, Jimmy will have to break the usual stereotypes about white rappers and prove his audience wrong.

Detroit's ghetto reality (drugs, sex and violence) is depicted with a great sense of realism.

Miz Korona stars as Vanessa, Jimmy's co-worker in the movie. Although the scene that opposes her to rapper Xzibit is amusing, it doesn't really enhance her qualities as an emcee. On the Detroit scene, Miz Korona is quite notorious for her wicked rapping style. That's why people call her "the Laila Ali of rap".

The other important lesson to learn from the movie is that respect and recognition have to be won step by step, little by little.

While one would be tempted to believe Wink who pretends to have a lot of inside connections that could lead Jimmy to the road of success, Future's plan is less risky and offers the aspiring emcee some well-built respect.

While Future aka David Porter represents Big Proof in real life, Wink refers to Detroit underground rapper Champtown, the first African American emcee to feature Eminem in his video, Do Da Dipity. Eminem would cut his ties with him when he feared Champtown was interested in Kim.

Alex cheats on Jimmy with Wink in the movie while Big O (King Gordy) is giving his interview.

Another character, emcee Bob, incarnates Marshall's former friend, known as 'Detroit's best kept secret', Bob Claus aka DJ Rec.

Although the role doesn't really flatter real life underground artist Bob Claus, it gives you some insight about the friends that surrounded Marshall Mathers in his early beginnings.

Alex's sluttish behavior will remind a lot of people about groupies who switch from one artist to another in order to obtain something (mostly money). Like Jimmy, she is ambitious, but she is not ready to make a sacrifice in terms of hard work to reach her goals. Her preference goes to modeling and if getting there implies having sex with somebody from the industry, she'll go ahead.

The sex scene with Jimmy in Detroit stamping is a mixture of tenderness in the middle of rough steel. It adds to the movie's realism.

In short, "8 Mile" is a lesson about life, dreams, courage and determination. Eminem's life can be a model for any of us who struggle to make it. Through "8 Mile", the talented rapper has proven that he can be a positive role model, especially for young people who are carrying a dream and who are dealing with the hardships of life.

In short, believe in the quality of your dreams, be determined, work hard and you'll get where you want to. If Marshall Mathers can, so can you. You just have to believe hard enough.

Controversies, dissentions and tensions around the "8 Mile" movie: some Detroit artists speak out

While a great majority of emcees are supportive towards Eminem and his "8 Mile" movie and grateful to Marshall for putting 8 Mile on the map, some others don't exactly feel the same way. Eminem is often reproached not to be supportive enough towards the Detroit hip hop Community since he rocketed to fame. When Eminem created his label, Shady Records, a lot of locals were hopeful in getting signed there, but as a matter of fact, more Atlanta rappers became part of the Shady Records team, which justifiably generated some bitterness in Detroit. Many Detroit rappers felt in a similar way about Shade 45, Eminem's free speech radio, because Detroit hip hop was left out for a major part in terms of representation.

In a 2009 interview I did with DJ Butter, the talented DJ expressed his biggest challenge was when Eminem and D12 turned against him:

> *When Eminem and D12 went against me: I just never understood how I can break bread with those guys before the big label deals and they couldn't break bread back. They made me out to be the bad guy. I was supporting Denaun Porter's music before he was making any rap money from Shady Records or any other platinum artists he deals with today. I paid those dudes to do songs for my label and they gave the tracks to Em's label. Last time I talk to him, he said he was gonna be a better DJ than me. I was there from the earlier days, when Eminem wasn't returning their calls. I always wanted the best for the Shady family and it's always been some bullshit politics. I have a conversation with Denaun on the phone, that will wake a lot of people up and I just didn't leak it. It's a G-Unit radio on Shade 45 and not D-12 radio and that's my point. But, I understood why Eminem walked away on the "8 Mile" movie.*

DJ Butter, Interview with Isabelle Esling, 2009

Back in the days, DJ Butter had an ongoing beef with D12. He had been setting a real effort on helping the emcees long before they all became famous. He was working on a mixtape in which all D12 emcees were featured. Barry Yett did the beat for the Shit Can Happen song, but he wasn't paid in return for his effort. Angry about the situation, the talented DJ prepared a diss in collaboration with Mister Clean and YBP, "Yo Band". DJ P-Dog backfired at DJ Butter with the I Got Beef mixtape, dissing DJ Butter in return. Bizarre also released a DJ Butter dissing track, Slow Your Role.

A lot of DJ Butter's arguments are justified. On the other hand, one can consider that, when an artist of Eminem's importance reaches the top, he also needs to expand his collaborations on a worldwide scale.

We can sense much more animosity in Detroit hip hop pioneers, the 5 ELA group's statements. In their opinion, Eminem's color played to his advantage. They see him as the traditional white American hero, like Silvester Stallone, who saves it all at the end:

> *America loves an underdog, especially white men who excel in things that traditionally thought of as "black".*

We all bore witness to Eminem's rise to fame and the depiction of the Detroit hip hop scene in the movie 8 Mile...where Philly had Rocky, a fictitious boxer, an underdog that went on to become the heavyweight champion of the world, Detroit boasts an underdog, Eminem, a real life white rapper who went on to dominate the rap game and has been called one of the best to ever pick up the mic. In the movie Rocky, Stallone's character was initially beaten by Apollo Creed. In "8 Mile", Eminem choked before sharpening his skills and coming back. That's where the similarities in these two movies end... Rocky we all know was fiction, and according to members of 5 Ela who came thru to offer real insight into the Detroit hip hop scene, the same can be said about what we think we know about Eminem and 8 Mile..." (5 ELA)

As a matter of fact, Mudd and Big Proof were very close. Mudd is the eye witness of Proof's murder at the CCC club in 7 Mile. D12's Kuniva said Mudd was responsible for Proof's death, which ignited a beef between both camps.

Local rapper Champtown considers that Eminem and his manager, Paul Rosenberg are prejudiced. He also accuses Eminem to have forgotten about his early rapping debuts and who introduced him to the rapping scene:

> *Em' should tell the truth," and "Em' jus' erased these five years out of his memory like they don't exist. It's not bitterness; it's just the truth should be heard. I respect Eminem, straight up. I've never seen anybody work so hard on a single verse. But I don't like it when muthafuckers don't give me my props.*
>
> Champtown, *Metro Times*

So, has Eminem gone too "Hollywood" since the release of his "8 Mile" movie?

In many ways, Eminem has proven to be deeply Detroit rooted. In a *Metro Times* interview that goes back to May 2009, Marshall Mathers shows some real interest in Detroit underground artists, he is trying to keep himself updated, but his busy working schedule sometimes keep him away from the actual happenings. The outstanding Detroit producer, Black Milk, gets a mention in this interview:

> *Well, honestly…Actually, I've been hearing a lot about… Black Milk?*

> *Yeah. I just recently heard a song … let me see, like last week, I think it was. But I haven't had a chance to really listen to a lot lately. It's only in the last couple of weeks that I stepped away from everything and put the pen down. So I've been like trying to get back into recent music. Because when I'm in work mode — when I'm actually writing lyrics and working on an album — I don't really listen to anybody else's records. That's just because I don't want to subconsciously take a flow or something from someone else, you know what I mean? I still want to make sure I sound like no one else when I rap. So I purposely stayed away a little bit from what's been going on in*

hip hop. And I'm trying to play catch up right now, especially with Detroit hip hop. So it's not really fair for me to give you a good answer on that as of right now. In other words, I might need a couple of more weeks to listen and then I'll be able to give a better answer on that.

Not only does Eminem seem concerned about the music scene in Detroit, he also pays attention to Motor City's automobile industry's difficulties:

Well, I don't really know how I see the future. I mean, I really wish I had an answer for what's going on here right now, you know? It really is kinda complicated for me when I look at it. But it just kinda pisses me off a little bit when people, like, I guess, refer to this city or look at this city as a whole. When you look at the crumbling auto industry ... [sighs] you see and hear people blaming the auto executives and shit like that for mismanaging the companies and, you know, putting money in their own pockets and taking too big of salaries and shit like that. But I don't know if people outside of Detroit realize, OK, yeah, that did happen and, yeah, they made some bad decisions. But in the long run, who is it affecting? Well, the real people of this city who are losing their jobs. They're the ones who are being affected by this daily. It's a really complicated situation because everyone is just pointing fingers right now. But the truth is it's fucking up the lives of real people here. You know what I mean?

From the Detroit hip hop scene's point of view, which is hoping for recognition on an international scale, some people are frustrated regarding Eminem's "lack of focus and artistic support towards the scene that made him" are sometimes understandable. However, pulling the race card on Eminem to explain his overwhelming success is just a lazy excuse.

In a CBS interview given in October 2010, Marshall Mathers recalls the atmosphere of the Detroit hip hop scene back in the day:

> *There was certainly like a rebellious, like, youthful rage in me.*
> *And there was also the fact of no getting away from fact that*
> *I am white and you know this is predominantly black music*
> *you know. And people were telling me 'You don't belong, like*
> *you're not going to succeed because you are this color.' Then you*
> *wanna show those people that you can and you will.*

Target your criticism in terms of competencies; race doesn't count when it comes to talent. Either you are talented, or not, period.

Eminem teaches Jimmy Kimmel how to rap

Back in the late 90s-early 2000s, Eminem used to incarnate the prototype of the American anti-hero with his lyrics, his numerous references to drugs, the use of the F word, his political rebellion, his anti-gay targets, Marshall Mathers probably became public enemy Number One in the eyes of the Establishment.

When he became famous, Eminem used to wear a mask-on stage, literally and during his public appearances, because he was using his alias the scary, psychopath Slim Shady character, to represent him. He was probably trying to protect his real self from the media's intrusion.

The release of the "8 Mile" movie played an essential role and contributed to help change people's perspective about the talented rapper. "8 Mile" introduced a lot of neophytes to the harsh world of battle rap. Now the mainstream public could see better where Eminem came from and the numerous challenges he had to face before he made it to the top. From a negative role model he transformed into a positive, youth appealing role model. Through his example, a lot of young people would learn a lot about motivation and determination. The phrase "You can do anything you set your mind to, man", taken out of the "Lose Yourself" song would become the strong motto for millions of people.

Marshall Mathers as a person, through his own life experiences, matured a lot. After his numerous drug abuses, he decided to become clean, which required a lot of willpower. He also felt more confident in showing his real side to the public to whom he confessed his weaknesses.

Eminem took it a step further when he went to the Jimmy Kimmel show in order to teach the famous presenter how to rap. In "Briefcase Joe", Eminem is poking fun at his own art: the hilarious show manages to make lyrical and flow techniques approachable to anybody. Rap music is complex, because you can hardly explain it, like you would take a classical partition and go from note to note. Rap isn't taught in schools. This is music you grow up into; you learn it in the streets of the ghetto.

You need to be a fine wordsmith and have a good sense of rhythm allied with a stormy flow and of course, possess a fine musical ear. Jimmy Kimmel gets caught in a verbal game, but Eminem wins at the end, because he gets unmasked.

People who are unfamiliar with the rap game also realized that some facts, like childhood humiliations are often amplified. An emcee is often turning personal weaknesses into strengths, which allow him to get admiration and approval from the supportive crowd.

We are also learning from Eminem's, in another 2009 Jimmy Kimmel appearance that attacks against famous people are often used for rhyming purposes. There is nothing really personal in these kinds of attacks. Like Eminem stated on TV, he didn't meet half of the persons he dissed in his songs.

This argument should help convince a lot of his opponents who usually tend to take each of Eminem's words too literally.

Rap music is a game. Know the rules and you will respect the player.

"Bending the words"

It is interesting to note that Eminem, who claims not to read poetry, but who has always been an avid dictionary reader, has a special gift when it comes to the usage, transform, and play with words and syllables.

He might not have been the ideal pupil at school, but his ability to handle the English language in a subtle way is undeniable:

> *I found that no matter how bad I was at school, like, and no matter how low my grades might have been at sometimes, I always was good at English*

In his CBS interview (October 2010), he explains a crucial rhyming secret that lies in the enunciation of words. Just by cutting a word in several syllables, you can let your creativity flow in a very interesting way:

> *It's just in the enunciation of it. Like, people say that the word 'orange' doesn't rhyme with anything and that kind 'a pisses me off because I can think of a lot of things that rhyme with orange.*
>
> *If you're taking the word at face value and you just say orange, nothing is going to rhyme with it exactly. If you enunciate it and you make it like more than one syllable? Orange, you could say like, 'I put my orange four-inch door hinge in storage and ate porridge with George.' So, you just have to figure out the science to breakin' down words.*

I find this statement very innovative and even brilliant, because even if many rappers are doing this exercise while emceeing, barely any of them came up with an interesting, explanatory statement such as this one about the art of rhyming. It allows the neophyte to catch the world of emceeing more easily. It gives you a glimpse of the battling world across 8 Mile.

Conclusion

You have entered the mind of a brilliant artist. Eminem has brought you into his world of full emotions and intense struggles. You have been traveling through the mind of a genius who took you apart with his rhymes; you've been feeling his pains, his sorrows and his happiness while listening to his music, because the Detroit emcee shared them with you.

Eminem is one of the rare artists to show true feelings and to speak his mind in his music. He is also one of the world's most creative hip-hop artists.

A great defender of the freedom of speech in America, rebellious in his mind, Eminem is never afraid to stand up for causes he finds right.

His avant-gardism in his way of expressing, his opposition political correctness truly impacted our contemporary society and will certainly help for things to move in a positive way. Today's youth is not ready to accept empty speeches packed with hypocrisy from the government anymore (Barack Obama's election in November 2008 fully proves this point) and the rapper's incisive words are more than a mere symbol.

Eminem is also the voice of the underground: Ghetto youths can relate to his songs. He also shows, through his own example, a new path of hope, because you "can do anything you set your mind to, man".

Eminem's life story, from the bottom to stardom simply shows that anything is possible, if you just believe.

But Eminem wouldn't be Eminem without the Detroit scene that fully shaped him. The rough Detroit hip hop scene has given birth to the most original, creative and dedicated artists. Hip hop ain't dead: it truly lives in the Big D—Detroit.

Bibliography

—ABC News, Sept15, 2000

—CBS News, Oct, 2010

—*Detroit Free Press* archive

—Eminem AKA, DVD

—Eminem, *Angry Blonde,* /Regan Books, 248 p.

—Isabelle Esling, Exclusive interview with Big Proof (January 2006), Interviews with Dogmatic, Rude of Iron Fist and Omar de Fati (2007), Interview with DJ Butter and rapper Mu (2009)

—Martin Huxley, *Eminem, Crossing The Line,* St Martin's Griffin, 133p

—*Metro Times,* archives

—KC TV5, News, November 2002

—*Oakland Press,* January 2012

—*Salon Com/ Entertainment*

—SOHH.COM. Paul Rosenberg on Eminem's Targets, July 2010

—*The Smoking Gun,* Archives

About the Author

Isabelle Esling graduated from the University of Metz, France, where she studied Liberal Arts/ Languages. She has been teaching modern foreign languages in public and private schools, mainly as a German and French teacher.

She has always had a passion for writing and music, black music in particular. She discovered Eminem in 2001 and has been very enthusiastic about the artist's great talent, which motivated her to write about him. It also motivated her to explore the Detroit hip hop scene, which is full of amazing artists.

In 2003, Gavin Sheridan, a technical writer and professional blogger, offered Miss Esling a position as a contributing writer for his blog, which got her started as a freelance music journalist. In 2005, with Gavin's help, she started The Eminem Blog where she discussed the artist Eminem, the Detroit hip hop scene and other hip hop related subjects.

Isabelle Esling has reviewed a wide range of CD's and interviewed some important artists such as Dina Rae, DJ Butter, Big Proof of D12, just to name a few. The Eminem Blog gained her a worldwide audience of readers. She has also contributed to numerous hip hop websites such as Music Mouth UK, Detroit Rap Com, Michigan Bands and D Townie.

In 2006, Miss Esling did a few interviews for Jason Matthews Detroit digital magazine *ILL Mag*. Through the years she developed her craft, increased her knowledge of hip hop culture and also commentated on various subjects such as spirituality, humanities, beauty and lifestyle, movies etc...she still writes at The Eminem Blog and shares her passion with her readers still today.

Isabelle Esling was born in Saint Avold, a little French town near the German border. Being a French national of German origin, she grew up bilingual speaking German-French in Freyming Merlebach, a tiny town very close to Saarbruecken. Her parents introduced her to classical music and jazz at a very early age and she showed some interest for writing and playing with words at a very early age.

As a young student , Isabelle settled in the French town of Metz, where she graduated. Some African students introduced her to James Brown and other remarkable artists like Barry White. In the early 90's she saw MC Hammer on TV for the first time, which triggered her passion for rap music.

Getting in touch with the African American culture for the very first time, Isabelle experienced the value of authenticity and truthfulness in a way that does not exist in White culture anymore. For this she is eternally grateful. This raised her political awareness to heights it had never known before. What kind of culture are we, allowing a system of institutionalized and perpetual inequality? Sadly, racism is not dead at all. This injustice has to stop, and I am proud that I am at least trying to do my tiny bit in this on-going struggle.

In 2006, Isabelle moved to London, England where she now resides.

ORDER FORM

WWW.AMBERBOOKS.COM

Fax Orders: 480-283-0991

Telephone Orders: 602-743-7211

Postal Orders: Send Checks & Money Orders Payable to:

    Amber Books

    1334 E. Chandler Blvd., Suite 5-D67, Phoenix, AZ 85048

Online Orders: E-mail: Amberbk@aol.com

____*Eminem & The Detroit Rap Scene,* ISBN#: 978-1-937269-26-5, $15.00
____*Too Young to Die, Too Old to Live: The Amy Winehouse Story,* ISBN#: 978-1-937269-28-9, $15.00
____*Lady Gaga: Born to Be Free,* ISBN#: 978-1-937269-24-1, $15.00
____*Nicki Minaj: The Woman Who Stole the World,* ISBN #: 978-1-937269-30-2, $15.00
____*Lil Wayne: An Unauthorized Biography,* ISBN#: 978-0-9824922-3-9, $15.00
____*Black Eyed Peas: Unauthorized Biography,* ISBN#: 978-0-9790976-4-5, $16.95
____*Red Hot Chili Peppers: In the Studio,* ISBN #: 978-0-9790976-5-2, $16.95
____*Dr. Dre In the Studio,* ISBN#: 0-9767735-5-4, $16.95
____*Kanye West in the Studio,* ISBN #: 0-9767735-6-2, $16.95
____*Tupac Shakur—(2Pac) In The Studio,* ISBN#: 0-9767735-0-3, $16.95
____*Jay-Z…and the Roc-A-Fella Dynasty,* ISBN#: 0-9749779-1-8, $16.95
____*Ready to Die: Notorious B.I.G.,* ISBN#: 0-9749779-3-4, $16.95
____*Suge Knight: The Rise, Fall, and Rise of Death Row Records,* ISBN#: 0-9702224-7-5, $21.95
____*50 Cent: No Holds Barred,* ISBN#: 0-9767735-2-X, $16.95
____*Aaliyah—An R&B Princess in Words and Pictures ,* ISBN#: 0-9702224-3-2, $10.95
____*You Forgot About Dre: Dr. Dre & Eminem,* ISBN#: 0-9702224-9-1, $10.95
____*Michael Jackson: The King of Pop,* ISBN#: 0-9749779-0-X, $29.95

Name:_____

Company Name:_____

Address:_____

City:_____State: _____Zip:_____

Telephone: (____)_____E-mail: _____

For Bulk Rates Call: 602-743-7211   ORDER NOW

Eminem	$15.00	❏ Check ❏ Money Order ❏ Cashiers Check
The Amy Winehouse Story	$15.00	❏ Credit Card: ❏ MC ❏ Visa ❏ Amex ❏ Discover
Lady Gaga	$15.00	
Nicki Minaj	$15.00	CC#_____
Lil Wayne: An Unauthorized Biography	$15.00	Expiration Date:_____
Black Eyed Peas	$16.95	
Red Hot Chili Peppers	$16.95	**Payable to: Amber Books**
Dr. Dre In the Studio	$16.95	Mail to: Amber Books
Kanye West	$16.95	1334 E. Chandler Blvd., Suite 5-D67
Tupac Shakur	$16.95	Phoenix, AZ 85048
Jay-Z…	$16.95	**Shipping:** $5.00. Allow 7 days for delivery.
Ready to Die: Notorious B.I.G.,	$16.95	
Suge Knight:	$21.95	**Total enclosed:** $_____
50 Cent: No Holds Barred,	$16.95	
Aaliyah—An R&B Princess	$10.95	
Dr. Dre & Eminem	$10.95	
Michael Jackson: The King of Pop	$29.95	

www.ingramcontent.com/pod-product-compliance
Lightning Source LLC
Chambersburg PA
CBHW051832090426
42736CB00011B/1764

* 9 7 8 1 9 3 7 2 6 9 2 6 5 *